INFORMATION STRUCTURE DESIGN FOR DATABASES

INFORMATION STRUCTURE DESIGN FOR DATABASES

A practical guide to data modelling

Andrew J. Mortimer

Butterworth-Heinemann Ltd
Linacre House, Jordan Hill, Oxford OX2 8DP

OXFORD LONDON BOSTON
MUNICH NEW DELHI SINGAPORE SYDNEY
TOKYO TORONTO WELLINGTON

First published 1993

British Library Cataloguing in Publication Data
A catalogue record for this book is available from the British Library

ISBN 0 7506 0683 5

Designed and typeset by the author
Printed and bound in Great Britain

'It's such a mistake, I always feel, to put one's trust in technique.'
George Smiley in John Le Carre's *The Looking Glass War.*

'When I use a word, it means just what I choose it to mean — neither more nor less.'
Humpty Dumpty in Lewis Carroll's *Alice Through the Looking Glass.*

To Sharon, without whose help this book would not have been possible.

Foreword

In writing this book, I was between the Scylla of academic theory of relational systems and the Charybdis of the practical job of designing working database information structures. To save myself I chose Charybdis. For this I make no apology, because there are already a great number of academic texts on this subject, and very few which attempt to present data modelling as an understandable and practical set of techniques for use in industry.

I have employed a great number of examples, case studies and diagrams in this book to help the reader understand this subject. I have developed some of these examples and case studies in teaching this subject to students. Others I have come across and learned from in my work in industry. I have tried to eliminate the mass of incomprehensible theory which makes so many people feel that data modelling is a difficult subject.

I do not believe, as a practical way of designing information structures for databases, that data modelling *is* a difficult subject. Far more difficult is learning from the user how the real-world information system operates, so that it can be modelled.

I would like to express my heartfelt gratitude to Sharon Geil, my wife, for her invaluable support and assistance in checking the manuscript for errors, both technical and grammatical. I would also like to thank Bob Large, John Hanlon and Tim Hutchings, all colleagues at the University of Glamorgan, for their help. Any errors which remain, of course, are wholly my own. Finally, I would like to thank all those — too numerous to thank personally — who have been instrumental in building my data modelling skills.

Andrew Mortimer
University of Glamorgan

Contents

List of Figures

Preface

In this preface, the reader will find the scope of this book, a note regarding the author's intentions in writing it, and a review of the method by which the author has tried to achieve these intentions.

Scope

This book is about practical data modelling. As well as covering the techniques of data modelling, it seeks to place these techniques in their context in the real world. It covers aspects of business systems and information systems in order that the reader may see why data modelling is so important and how data modelling impacts on the organisations that employ databases in their day-to-day operations. It also examines the process of developing information systems and attempts to place data modelling in its correct place within this process.

The techniques described in this book are primarily used for developing data models which will be implemented in relational database management systems. The advent of object-oriented databases does not, however, invalidate more than a small part of these techniques, and the prevalence of relational database management systems in the business and organisational world suggest that a relational approach, for the time being at least, is much more likely to be of benefit to the reader.

Some of the techniques associated with data modelling have arisen from the theoretical study of data modelling from the mathematician's point of view. Normalisation, for example, is a technique commonly advocated for data modelling. Normalisation has only a brief discussion in this book, because it is seen by the author as one of the greatest sources of confusion in those who are studying and trying to understand data modelling for the first time. Normalisation is presented, not as a technique of data analysis, but as a way of confirming and checking data designs once they have been developed using graphical design techniques. Other techniques and methods have not been discussed for the same reason — to keep the scope of the book within the remit of practical data modelling and to provide the reader with only such material as is necessary to do the job, and to be able to apply techniques to new and unexpected situations.

This book aims to make the subject of data modelling accessible to those who have neither a mathematical nor a scientific interest in data modelling. For this reason, many of the aspects of data modelling found in more technical or scientific books on the subject will not be found in this book.

Intentions

It is one of the intentions of the author to deliver a readable, informative, and entertaining explanation of data modelling for the beginner. The explanations of the techniques of data modelling make as few assumptions as possible about the prior knowledge of the reader. However, the book also contains a number of practical techniques which the author has not previously seen in any book on the subject of data analysis and design. For this reason the book will also be of interest to those who already have a grounding in the subject, and who may already have applied it in the business or organisational context.

The book also provides a variety of examples and case study materials, exploring not only the basic structures of information in organisations, but also considering a number of unusual or elegant solutions. It is also the intention of the author to communicate the mind-set of the good data analyst, demonstrating how an enquiring mind and an excellent relationship with the user can lead to a deeper understanding of the organisational needs and an improved, more elegant solution.Thus, the book is intended for

- business or organisational management or staff who wish to understand more about the way information is analysed and stored in databases
- students on computer or information systems courses of study who wish to gain a practical insight to their studies of data analysis and design
- students on non-computer courses who wish to obtain an understanding of information analysis and database design as it will impact on their chosen professions. A large number of courses now include aspects of information systems in their coverage for the simple reason that computer information systems impact on nearly all aspects of life and nearly all professional disciplines
- data analysts who already understand and use data modelling techniques in their jobs as developers of information systems,

and who wish to obtain a deeper or broader view of the tricks and techniques which can be used to improve database designs or to produce more elegant, more efficient or simpler data structures.

Method

This book is divided into four main areas, to provide the reader with a detailed examination of the techniques of practical data modelling, and also with the context within which data modelling occurs in the real world of systems development and organisational information needs. The data analyst's job is not carried out in isolation, and it is the author's belief that a good data analyst will possess many other skills and knowledge than those required to create a data model.

In the first few chapters, the organisational context is considered: what information is, what qualities it must have to be useful, how this information affects the organisations that use it. Information is a vital and central resource for all organisations. To illustrate this point the kinds of system that require well-designed information structures are reviewed.

Following on from the business or organisational context are the chapters on the techniques of data modelling; covering entity relationship modelling, data flow diagramming, the use of entity life histories and the use of the logical data dictionary. These four comprise the main techniques of data modelling as put forward in this book.

In the section which starts to explain the techniques of data modelling we look at sinks and sources of data, flows of data, processes, data stores (both as file storage locations for data and as being analogous to the entity in the Entity Relationship Model). The ideas of the conservation of data, multi-level Data Flow Diagrams, naming conventions and the link with Entity Relationship Models are all explored. Entities and their unique identifiers, types of entity, the attributes or characteristics of entities, relationships between entities, the degree of relationship between entities and membership of relationships are all explained.

Following the chapters on technique, there are three chapters in which these data modelling techniques are applied to actual organisational or business problems. We see the development of a data model for a five-a-side football league, a firm involved in obtaining and managing bookings for musical acts and finally a more complex model for a shipping company.

The author would like to stress at this point that reading through and understanding the case study chapters is an essential part of learning practical data modelling from this book. It is for this reason that the case studies appear as chapters integrated in the flow of chapters, rather than appendices tacked on at the end. These case studies demonstrate the application of the techniques described in earlier chapters, taking the reader step-by-step through the process of data analysis, from the first proposals by the user or user organisation, through the investigation of the environment, the first drafts of the data model and refining that model by talking to the user. At the end of each of the case study chapters, the final data dictionary is presented.

Following the chapters which demonstrate the application of the techniques of data modelling are the chapters on the systems development context. In these chapters the author describes the systems development task and attempts to place data modelling in the context of systems development. Data modelling is not just about designing database structures for the development of new databases. It is also to do with the evolutionary development of existing systems, the proper and efficient use of the database and the information it contains. A good data analyst will also have knowledge and skills which impact on the data model and the database: security of information, and persuading corporate management to adopt a sensible and strategic attitude to information systems.

Finally, following the last chapter, the reader will find a reading list of books which may be useful in deepening the knowledge and skills obtained in the main text, a glossary of terms and an appendix which explains the position of data modelling within the systems development methodology SSADM, and where differences exist between the techniques defined by SSADM and those put forward in this book.

The understanding of the theory behind a technique is necessary to allow the practitioner to apply the technique in situations which are unusual or previously not encountered. The over-stressing of theory has been a problem in the past, putting off those who simply want to understand how to apply techniques in practice. It is hoped that this book pitches theory at the level needed by the intelligent and adaptable practitioner, and no higher.

The practical use of data modelling techniques to verify the design of a database is not at all difficult. It is a matter of common sense, once the simple fundamental principles of the relational data model are understood.

The book stresses the need for the designer to be aware of the underlying structure of the enterprise's environment, information needs and business processes. The user community is explored, looking at the need for a good understanding of user expectations and how to manage those expectations. Some ideas are presented on how to approach user contact and how to use the user as verifier of the data model.

Above all, it is hoped that the reader will appreciate firstly, that data modelling is an integrated and coordinated use of many data modelling techniques, each of which in isolation is a poor tool. Secondly, that data analysis and design, and data modelling are highly relevant and very practical disciplines which will be in greater and greater demand as information systems technology advances.

Objectives

At the end of the book, the reader should be able to:

- Analyse a data requirement from simple sources such as documents and discussions with users and apply the techniques of data modelling to arrive at an elegant, workable and effective design.
- Produce the full set of documentation for a simple database requirement.
- Understand what is needed for a full and complete database design.
- Understand that data modelling uses:

  Entity Relationship Models

  Entity Life Histories

  Data Flow Diagrams

  Logical Data Dictionaries

  Well normalised tables

  and that all these techniques are used in a coordinated and integrated way.
- Understand that data modelling techniques all require a good understanding of the organisation, how it operates and what data it uses now and may use in the future.

- Understand the rewards of having access to timely, accurate, reliable and meaningful information about all aspects of the organisation.
- Understand the consequences of inaccurate, out-of-date, incomprehensible or inaccessible data.
- Understand the benefits of using up-to-date techniques and technology to create and maintain a database.

Features

- Extensive use of diagrams
- Bullet point checklists
- Style notes highlighted in text
- Clear explanations
- Frequent examples
- Worked case studies, many taken from actual case histories
- End of chapter summaries
- Glossary of technical terms
- Comprehensive index

CHAPTER 1

DATA ANALYSIS IS EASY

☐ **Brief Overview of Data Modelling — Tables are about Things — Uniquely Identifying Things — Table Columns as Information — Relationships — New Concepts**

Tables

The fundamental concept behind data modelling starts with the idea of a table. Most people are familiar with the idea of a table, where information is presented in rows and columns. One way of looking at data modelling is to

Table: Person				
Surname	Forename	Height(cm)	Weight(kg)	Date Of Birth
Smith	Anna	161	62	12/7/1949
Evans	Peter	181	85	7/10/1962
Jackson	John	179	74	1/5/1968

see it as a process of determining what tables are needed to store all the information that will be held in the database. It is really as simple as that. Each row of a table represents one incidence of the thing that the table is about.

In the above table, we are recording information about a thing called 'person'. In each column we are storing certain facts about the person. These are items of information which 'belong' to the person — characteristics or attributes of the person. Each column contains the same kind of information, each row represents the existence of one person in our database. Each intersection between a row and a column contains one item of information about the thing which occupies the row.

Data analysis abounds with jargon — in data modelling a thing is called an entity. If you look up entity in a dictionary, you will find that it means 'a thing'. An entity is any *thing* about which we wish to store information.

This kind of database is a very simple one. There are many such databases in the world — very few of them on a computer. There are a number of rules with which most people would agree, when creating such a table, for example:

- the table should have a name which describes what it is about
- each column must contain the same kind of information
- each column should have one name
- each row must be able to be uniquely identified
- each intersection of row and column must contain only one data item
- each item of information should be stored only once in the table

Such a database could easily be kept on index cards, for example (many databases are), but such a database can also be kept in a computer. Computers are very good at holding such information reliably, and at moving data about very quickly and efficiently. What is more, the computer can present the information to us in any way that we want, without us having to worry about how it is stored. It is not surprising, then, that many organisations use computers to hold and manipulate large databases.

Computers tend to be good with tables, which in a computer are often called files. A file has a number of records, like the rows in our tables. The fields in a computer record are like the cells in our column.

Relationships

With a large database, there are many tables, which have relationships between them. For example:

Table : Car					
Registration	Colour	Engine Number	Capacity	Model	Manufacturer
A456TYU	Blue	876574674764	1300	Escort	Ford
C234ERT	Red	365500009878	1400	Nova	Vauxhall

Table : Service			
Registration	Date of Service	Serviced By	Type of Service
A456TYU	12/12/91	Autofix Garages	12000
A456TYU	18/3/92	Smiths	24000
C234ERT	17/3/91	Autofix Garages	12000

You will see that the relationship between the two tables above is that *cars* may have many *services* and that each service was of one car. (Another way of putting it is that services repeat for each car.) The fact that there are many services for each car is obvious, surely? This concept — one to many — between two tables is a fundamental concept in computer database analysis and design. Yet it is not a complex or difficult idea.

The information in the two tables *car* and *service* could be rewritten as:

Table : Services and Capacity				
Registration	Date of Service	Type of Service	Serviced By	Capacity
A456TYU	12/12/91	12000	Autofix Garages	1300
C234ERT	17/3/91	12000	Autofix Garages	1400
A456TYU	18/3/92	24000	Smiths	1300

In this table, we can see the capacity of the car as well as the services that have been carried out on it. This is useful information to know, perhaps, for the mechanic who is carrying out a new service on the car. However, it would not be sensible to keep engine capacity permanently in the table for services — for two reasons. Firstly, it is simply a waste of space, and secondly, if we have to change the capacity of the car for some reason (because it was entered incorrectly, for example), we would waste time by changing it twice, in two different places. If, due to an oversight, the information was changed in only one of the two places, we would have inconsistent information in our database about the car.

So, in data modelling, we design the database to hold each item of information only once.

To show the relationship between two tables, there are a number of things we must do. Firstly, in order to allow the services to be associated with a car, the car must have a unique identification — in this case the registration number. The registration number must be included somewhere in the table called *service* — so that we know which car the service was for. The unique identification is sometimes called *the unique key*, and when we place the key of one table in another table to show the link between the two, it is called a *foreign key*.

New Concepts

This brief introduction to the basic ideas of data modelling has covered many of the fundamental principles necessary for understanding this subject:

- One to many
  Where a single row in one table is associated with many rows in another table — a *car* is associated with many *services.*
- Unique identifier
  The attribute which uniquely identifies the entity — such as the registration number of the car.
- Foreign key
  The placing of the identifier or key of one table into another table to show the link between the two things. The registration number of the *car* was included in the table *service* to show which car the service was for.
- Elimination of redundant duplication
  Arranging the tables in such a way that the same information is never *unnecessarily* included more than once.
- Attributes owned by entities
  The named characteristics of the thing which we want to record — such as the columns *height* and *weight* in the table *person.*

All further details of data modelling are concerned with the design of the database for:

- elimination of as much duplication as possible
- easiest possible access between tables
- elimination, as much as possible, of any possibility of corruption of the information.

Data analysis asks among others, the following questions:

- What will each of our tables be called?
- What thing will each table be about?
- What columns will we need to store the information?
- Are there any rules about what can be put into a column?
- What are the best identifiers to allow us to get from one table to another?

As you read and understand this book, you will find that the explanations you have read in this section may seem a little simplistic. That is quite possible. The explanations given above are written in layman's terms, and database analysis is far more than this. But if you have understood the concepts above, you should have no difficulty in understanding any aspect of data modelling.

Data modelling is a combination of common sense — as in the explanations of the simple tables above — and a good understanding of the information needs of the organisation which is to use the database.

Data Analysis is Easy

Summary

- Data modelling is about tables
- Tables are made up of rows and columns

  Each row holds one occurrence of the thing the table is about

  Each column holds one item of information about the thing
- Tables are related by putting the reference number of one table into another table

CHAPTER 2

DATA AND INFORMATION

☐ **The Nature of Information — Cost and Value of Information — Uses and Presentation of Information — Difference between Data and Information — Need for Data Modelling — Impact of Good Design — Fourth Generation Environments**

What is Information?

Information is facts. For the purposes of data modelling, information can be seen as the facts about a business or organisation which are used to operate that organisation and to make decisions about the activities of that organisation.

In recent decades it has become more clearly understood by both computer systems professionals and the management of all businesses and organisations that information is the life blood of business or organisational activity. The Europeans have coined a word for this subject, which is found in various forms in Europe — informatics or informatiques — and which is beginning to appear in Britain as the term *information systems*.

That the power of information has been recognised, there is no doubt. There still remains the question, however, as to whether we are clear that it is a field of study and effort in its own right. There are today many professionals who regard themselves not as computer professionals, nor as business professionals, but as information systems professionals. These people seek to use computer and information technology (IT) techniques, in conjunction with their knowledge of business systems, to provide the business or organisation with the best possible information.

This means understanding the business, understanding what it does and why it does it, what information is needed for the proper running of the organisation, and analysing this information and designing data structures so as to allow the information to be held, without redundancy, duplication or wasted space, in a computer database.

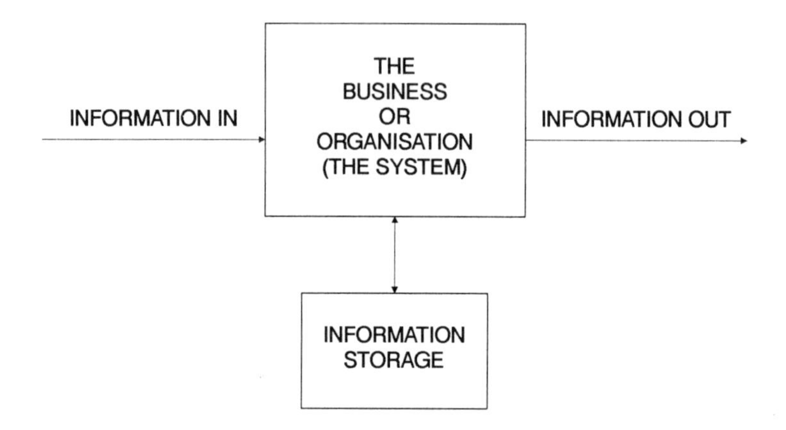

Figure 2-1 The Business or Organisation

A business or organisation, like any other system, has inputs, outputs, processes and storage of information.

All businesses and organisations keep information about their own activities and their interaction with the world around them. This information concerns such things as:

- customers and clients
- staff
- invoices issued to customers
- parts and prices
- services and rates
- bills to be paid

- delivery notes
- vehicles
- bookings

The information which is held about these things must be accurate to be of use. The ability of the organisation and its management to access this information quickly and reliably is critical.

Cost and Value of Information

Cost and value are not the same thing. Cost is what you have to pay (in money, time, resources or trouble) to get something into your possession. Value is the benefit to you (by resale, use or otherwise) once you have the something in your possession. Neither cost nor value can always be measured in financial or numeric terms, although other terms are not usually respected by management. Unquantifiable benefits can accrue from information, but some measure is normally necessary in order to judge proper action.

It doesn't usually make sense to pay more for something than it is worth to you. To do this too often will inevitably lead to disaster, since there is more going out than is coming in. It is more usual to try and make sure that more is coming in than is going out. This way leads to happiness.

'Annual income twenty pounds, annual expenditure nineteen nineteen six, result happiness. Annual income twenty pounds, annual expenditure twenty pound ought and six, result misery.' Mr Micawber in Charles Dickens' *David Copperfield* knew what he was talking about.

It clearly does not make sense, then, for an organisation to spend more money and resources on gathering and keeping information than the information is worth. This is throwing away money. The organisation is in a much better position if it is employing information to great benefit, information which is easy and inexpensive to obtain and to keep. It is important for the health of any organisation for it to keep this transaction in the black.

- How do we know how much it is costing us to obtain information?
- How much does it cost us to keep the information?

- What benefits are we getting from the information which we are keeping?

The answers to these questions are extremely important. As with any other management issue, it is perfectly possible for a company to survive without sensible and controlled management of its information. If it is able to survive and even to thrive without proper information resource management, how much more successful would it be if good information resource management were put in place?

The cost of obtaining information can arise in many ways:

- Communications costs : telephone, telex, satellite fees
- Wages and salaries of gatherers

The cost of keeping information may involve:

- The cost of purchase and maintenance of hardware
- The cost of keeping information secure
- The cost of housing and protecting equipment

The maintenance costs of data are made up of:

- Verifying the ongoing accuracy of information
- Changing inaccurate information
- Obtaining new information to keep the existing information accurate

Different organisations exist in environments with quite different rates of change. Businesses, for example, involved in tax law may have to change their policies every year at the start of the tax year. Other organisations may exist in even more dynamic information environments. The cost of maintaining an accurate database will be greater if the information changes more frequently.

Data and Information Differ

Data and information can be defined as quite different things. Data could be defined as raw figures, in any form at all, often represented by a mass of characters or codes on paper or in electronic or magnetic form. Information is by definition informative. It has meaning. Data does not have to have meaning to an observer.

A mass of data may not be able to be converted into information because it has become corrupted in some way or because it never had meaning in the first place. Information may be wrong or inaccurate or out of date, but it still informs. The basic difference is that information has *meaning* — semantic content.

This may seem to some people to be an arbitrary or unimportant distinction. Indeed, there are many cases where the words data and information are used interchangeably or as synonyms for each other. Indeed, from now on in the text, you may well find the two terms used loosely, where the distinction is unimportant. Sometimes, it is unimportant to make the distinction between data and information, but more often, it is vital to understand the difference.

Computers are not interested in information. No storage system is interested in information. People are interested in information, but have no interest in data. The data, if you like, is potential information and the job of an information system (by which is meant both the hardware, the software and the people which are part of the information system) is to supply information to decision makers and operational staff in a form which is of use to them. The data has no intrinsic value of itself. Once converted into information its value can be enormous.

Quality of Information

The quality of information is extremely important. Quality has been defined as giving people what they wanted when they came to you. This is quite different from giving them what they asked for. It is all very well to say : But I've given you what you asked for — it's not my fault if you didn't know what you wanted! The customer, as the saying goes, is always right, and those customers who are happy with you and with what you supply will come back for more. If you want to keep your customers — a customer being anyone who comes to you for anything, then you must make it your job to sort out what they really wanted from what they said they wanted if these two are different. They usually are.

In the systems development field there is a higher degree of discrepancy between what was wanted and what was delivered than in any other field of human endeavour. This may have something to do with the divide between the theoreticians and the practitioners of the world or may just be a symptom of the relative youth of the IS (information systems) development industry. Quality of information is giving the users what they wanted. When a user asks for an item of information, the user wants the information which is received from the information system to have four essential characteristics: users want their information to be:

- timely
- accurate
- relevant
- meaningful

Timeliness of Information

Information is no good if it is out of date. When a sales manager asks for the value of sales in the month of December, it is of no use to supply December's sales less the sales in the last week because they haven't been received from the branches yet. The information should have a specified timeliness and within that timescale, should be accurate. The timescales, of course, must be specified.

The information supplied to an alarm system about the state of a heart patient on a life support machine in an intensive care unit is no use if it is half an hour out of date. Information supplied to a fail-safe shut down controller from the core of a nuclear reactor is no good if it is seconds out of date. In these cases the timeliness of the information is nearly absolute. In other cases a delay is often inevitable and acceptable. The information supplied must however be within the timeliness factor specified. If it is not, it is inaccurate.

Accuracy of Information

In many situations a tolerance for accuracy exists, and is expected and acceptable. The accuracy should be, for example, within plus or minus one per cent or plus or minus ten per cent, or accurate to within an absolute amount. This must be specified, and must be adhered to.

Of all the failures in supplying quality information that are possible, the failure to supply accurate information is the worst. There is no more serious problem in an environment than management or staff taking action or making decisions on the basis of information which is not accurate, *but which is believed to be accurate.* If a user knows that a certain source of information is inaccurate, the decision can be deferred or not made at all. Even though this will inevitably mean that the organisation's faith in the information system will deteriorate, leading quite possibly to a complete rejection of these systems, at least it is known that the information is poor. To take action on false information which is believed to be true will usually be disastrous.

It is vital that the information system maintains its reputation for supplying accurate information. Upon this reputation rests the acceptance of the system by the users. Information supplied by the system must not only be accurate, but must be seen to be accurate. It will only take a few incidents of errors in action or decision caused by inaccurate information for the use of the system by the users to be impaired.

Relevance of Information

Every day, tons of paper are wasted in organisations which use computerised data processing. There is a phenomenon known as the regular or production report, which is produced on a regular basis — daily, weekly or monthly, perhaps — and delivered to the user whether or not the user has asked for it. While many such reports are neccessary and are a useful reference for the user, many are of no interest and are consigned to the waste bin or are left on the side of the desk as a kind of ornament. Furthermore, many reports include an inseperable mix of information which is relevant to the user's task and information which is of no use whatever to the user. If the user has no interest in the information, if the information has no relevance to the user's job or task, the information is ignored and does not inform.

Meaningfulness of Information

Information is useful when it is understood. When information (however accurate and timely it may be) is not understood, or even worse, misunderstood, it is arguable as to whether the user would have been better off without any information at all, rather than making important decisions on the basis of incorrectly understood information.

Thus the presentation of the information is vital for the information system to be successful.

Availability of Information

In many databases, there exists data in the data structures which is potential information. This data is there, but if it cannot or is not brought into the light of day, it is wasted. There are several issues here. It may be that the data is inaccessible and despite management desire to see the information and despite the fact that the raw data is in the database, management has no access to it. It may be that information is available from the database, but management (or any other person in the organisation who may be interested in or need the information) is not aware of its existence or availability.

Not so very long ago, the European managing director of a small but very dynamic software company had just received a copy of a new piece of software. This software was capable of taking a mass of raw data in relational format and displaying it graphically — as graphs, bar charts and so on — in any permutation the user desired. For example, the manager could ask for sales in the previous year by branch. The same sales figures could be displayed by product, or by classes of product. By moving down to a specified class of product, the manager could again display by branch. The company's products could be sold for different manufacturers' computers and this too could be displayed. The managing director was overheard saying: 'If only I had had this facility a year ago, I would have seen trends earlier that I didn't find out about until too late, and most, if not all, of our redundancies last month might have been prevented'.

This is an example of the availability of information having a major impact on the organisation.

Importance of Data Modelling

The use of data modelling techniques can make a tremendous difference to the availability of information. In another organisation, a programmer was asked to use a fourth generation language to produce a report for management on wastage within branches. This wastage was to be listed by branch and was to include items such as damaged stock, stock returned by customers, faulty stock items and so on.

A fourth generation language is usually very good at producing such reports, and it was anticipated that only a matter of hours of work would be required to produce a report which was satisfactory to the manager concerned.

When the programmer started work, it was found that every one of the data items representing the various columns were in a different database in the company's computer systems and that in none of the databases was *branch* a key field. The report took days to produce because of the complexity of locating and sorting the information. The database design for the information required was extremely poor.

This lack of good design was not because there was no-one available who had understood the need for good design. Nor was it because there was no one available who had the skills to produce a good design. It was because the database had grown over a period of several years, driven not by a database philosophy but by the individual and short-term needs of individual programs and subsystems which were written as needed.

The increasing tendency for businesses, and those people who supply information systems to those businesses, to employ database management systems (DBMS) and fourth generation environments (4GE) makes the need for good data modelling practices even more important. A database management system is a special piece of computer software which controls and organises and allows access to a database. A fourth generation environment is composed of software (usually including a database management system) which allows the speedy creation of information processing and retrieval systems. Neither of these facilities can operate effectively unless the database is well-designed.

We have examined the importance of information, how information about the outside world and about the day-to-day activities is critical for the proper running and management of any organisation or business. The skills of data modelling centre on this importance.

Data and Information

Summary

- Data is

  raw facts
  unstructured
  gives no information and
  is of no use to the person in the organisation

- Information is useful and meaningful
- Information has a cost
- The cost of information is equal to

  the cost of obtaining it
  plus
  the cost of maintaining it

- The cost of maintaining data varies with the rate of change of the natural world about which data is kept
- Maintaining data requires

  storage
  update

- Information must be

  timely
  accurate
  relevant
  meaningful

- The degree of timeliness and accuracy required by the system will directly affect the cost of obtaining the data
- The quality of presentation of the data as information has a direct effect on the cost of the information

CHAPTER 3

BUSINESS ANALYSIS

- **The Information Environment — Some Types of Information System — The User Community — Understanding Expectations —Managing Expectations — User Contact — User as Verifier of the Data Model**

The Information Environment

Data modelling is used to analyse the information needs and structures of an organisation in order to produce a data model for a database. This is a very practical skill, and no examination of practical data modelling could be complete without reviewing the importance of information systems to businesses and organisations. In this chapter, we will look at the kind of information systems that are found in organisations. We will also look at the relationship between the data analyst and designer and the user — this creature so often misunderstood by computer professionals — and how this relationship allows the exchange of knowledge which is necessary for the creation of a successful data model.

Databases could be said to be the heart and soul of any enterprise. An enterprise may be a profit-making organisation, or may be an organisation which does not exist to make a profit for its own sake but to serve society. An enterprise is an organisation which has purpose and direction, and in order to achieve this purpose will almost certainly keep information about itself, about its activities, its resources and about the world in which it operates.

The information which it holds will be in one way or another a model — a copy or representation — of reality. A company which keeps records of the orders which have been placed with it for goods or services does so in order to control and fulfil these orders. The information about the orders which is held by the organisation — whether in a computer-based system or in paper-based records — is a logical copy of what is going on in the real world. The closeness of the fit between the model and the reality will directly impact upon the success of the organisation.

Types of Information System

The uses to which computer systems are put are very varied. Some computer systems have databases as an integral part of their function, some systems do not. Some computer systems which have a database at their core are to do with modelling a real world environment. For example, a traffic light controller is a computer system, but it has no database as such. A scientific system which holds the results of experiments in order to produce statistical analyses is a computer system with a database, but does not as such provide a model of a real world environment. Working with data analysis is normally for the purpose of creating an information system — a computer-based system which accepts, manipulates and reports information for the purpose of managing and controlling an organisation or enterprise environment.

Such information systems include:

- Accounting systems

  Nominal or general ledger
  Purchase ledger
  Sales ledger
- Inventory or stock management systems
- Order management systems
- Manufacturing or production systems

All of these types of information systems have to be produced using some form of data analysis and database design.

Accounting Systems

Of all the systems which exist in industry, commerce and the enterprise community, accounting systems are probably the most common. Even those organisations which do not obtain their revenue from their customers directly will have a need for internal accounting records. Staff have to be paid. They must be paid the right amounts and at the right time.

The resources of the organisation — materials, stationery, premises and equipment — have to be bought or leased and have to be paid for. The records relating to all the financial transactions of an enterprise have to be recorded with absolute accuracy. Errors or inaccuracies in accounting are one of the surest ways of guaranteeing disaster. Management must know how much is being spent, how much money there is in the bank, how much cash is available for purchases, where cash is coming from and when it will arrive. These and many other financial facts are the basis on which management monitors and controls the activities of an organisation.

Accounting systems are used to prepare sets of accounts for the purposes of management reporting, for tax purposes, for budgeting and planning purposes. Accounts used for these purposes are generally referred to as general ledger accounts or nominal ledger accounts.

Financial transactions between a trading enterprise and its customers are called accounts receivable (also known as sales ledger). These accounts record transactions owed to the enterprise or received by the enterprise. Such accounts will often include elements of credit control — deciding how much you are prepared to let people owe you and how you are going to behave towards people who have outstanding debts with you.

This part of a financial system is also involved with invoicing — a vital part of many organisations. Invoices sent out late will adversely affect the cash flow of an organisation, and a high proportion of invoicing errors (which customers will normally leap on as an excuse for delaying payment) can cause not only cash-flow problems, but can also tie up many of your staff in sorting out problems and can cause ill-will between the organisation and its customers.

Financial information about what your organisation owes to other people and organisations is often referred to as accounts payable (also known as purchase or bought ledger). These accounts control who you owe money to (and why), when you will pay them, how you will pay them and how much you will pay them. Often such systems will have built in policies for paying as late as you can, firstly to keep cash flow as healthy as possible and secondly to ensure that you really have received the goods or services that your suppliers claim that you have received and that they are of a proper quality.

Inventory and Stock Management

Many organisations keep stocks of parts or goods which are used to build other finished goods or equipment, or for direct distribution to customers. This stock of goods or parts must be controlled and managed because it represents a major investment, because it is a valuable resource and because a failure in supply of a particular item may cause serious problems with the activities of the organisation or may cause problems with customer goodwill.

The absence of a part which is needed to make something will hold up the activity of making that thing. The whole of a production system can grind to halt because of the non-availability of something quite small and cheap.

The organisation's customers may terminate their relationship if goods which they are used to getting quickly are not available. They will go to someone whose inventory systems are more effective. Even worse, customers who receive goods they have not asked for, or do not receive goods they have asked for or who receive damaged or the wrong type of goods will not stay with their supplier long.

The control and management of the inventory has many aspects, including the reorder level (ROL), the economic order quantity (EOQ), the storage location and space available in the various bins or locations and the lead time for delivery. All of these aspects of control require accurate and timely information. The funds spent on stocks, the value of stocks, the cost of keeping and maintaining stocks and the money obtained for stock items are all financial information which will be reflected in the accounts.

Order Management Systems

Many organisations supply goods or services to other organisations or to individuals. Customers register needs and requirements with the organisation by placing an order or orders. These orders must be controlled and managed, and this control and management has many aspects and can be quite complex. An order for goods may require those goods to be purchased from outside for resale. It may require the goods to be produced, such as in a bakery or a manufacturing environment.

The orders currently in the books may drive the production process of an organisation. It is often the case that only a part of all the goods or services in one particular order can be filled, and the rest of the order must remain current until it is completely filled. It may be that some of the goods or services ordered are no longer available, and that part of an order which refers to such goods and services must be somehow dealt with.

The state of an order must be controlled and monitored. The customer will often contact a supplier for information on the status of an order, and if your organisation can give the customer accurate information quickly and competently, it builds confidence and goodwill between the organisation and its customers. Orders which are part filled must be checked periodically to see if the rest of the order has been filled or, even better, some mechanism exists to remind the organisation about the order when the necessary goods have arrived.

Another aspect of order management concerns staged or phased orders. An order for a complex deliverable may be delivered in stages on given dates. This kind of order must be carefully and accurately recorded and the information about the order must be available within the system.

Manufacturing Systems

Some organisations — those which produce goods by a manufacturing or construction process — will have a system to ensure the smooth flow of work in progress through the manufacturing or production system. Such systems, although not as common as financial accounting systems for example, are vital to the proper running of organisations which use them. These systems interface with the inventory system to record part finished goods and to control the smooth supply of parts or materials which are needed for the production process.

Manufacturing systems often involve a large number of complex and varied processes. In such situations, the system will have to utilise the people, processes and equipment in the manufacturing environment as efficiently as possible, through a process of scheduling. The less wastage of materials and time there is and the more efficiently a valuable machine or expensive process is used, the better off the organisation is. The more smoothly work in progress moves from one process to the next, the less wastage will occur.

Data Driven Systems

All systems are, in the final analysis, driven by data or information. This means that the data structures within the organisation must be carefully thought out and must work effectively. The information requirements of a system can change — sometimes subtly, sometimes dramatically — as a result of changes within the organisation, changes to its policies or ways of doing business and changes to the world outside. Such changes are becoming more and more important. The pace and rate of change in organisations differs depending on the nature of the organisation, what it does and who it does it for.

The rate of change, however, in nearly all organisations, is getting faster and faster with every passing decade, year or month — and in some organisations, every day. For this reason it is important that the data structures inside the organisations systems are designed well so that they can change with the organisation.

The User Community

The word *user* is familiar to most people in the field of computing or information systems. The data analyst will always be in contact with the user community when carrying out the job of data analysis and database design.

The user community will supply the understanding of how the organisation operates and what information the organisation needs to carry out its activities. The user community will review and criticise the database design, either accepting it as a workable and satisfactory solution or offering suggestions for improvement. It is the user community which will use the systems based on the database design and who will give the data analyst and designer either a 'thumbs up', by using the system happily and efficiently, or a 'thumbs down' by partly or wholly rejecting the system. The user community will also be the main drivers of the continuing evolution of the information system, requesting and verifying changes to the database and the functionality of the system in response to the changing needs of the organisation and the information world in which it resides.

In recent years, the focus on the user has become greater when designing, developing and changing computer systems. It is about time too. For far too long, systems analysts and systems developers have tried to impose on the users their own view of the user's organisation.

The user is the only person who knows what is needed. This, perhaps, is a rather sweeping and bald statement, and could do with a little qualification. The analyst's job is to extract from the user the specification or description of the system that the user needs. What the user says is wanted and what is actually wanted may not be the same thing at all. It is very difficult for someone who is unfamiliar with computer systems and systems development to put into words what they want. This problem is made far worse by the tendency for systems people to wrap up their job and their field of expertise with jargon.

The data analyst may well be able to clarify the structures of the information in the user's environment by applying the disciplines and techniques of data analysis and design. In this sense, the data analyst acts as an operational research role, not imposing views upon the users but, while using caution, helping the users to improve their own views. The important thing to

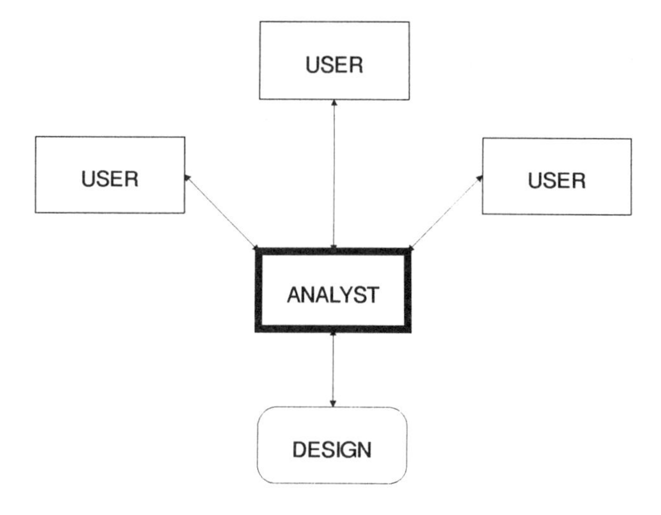

Figure 3-1 The Analyst's Interaction With Users

remember is that the analyst is there to listen to the user, to understand what the user is doing and to give the user what they need.

Users may be individuals in the operational area of the organisation — a clerk or worker on the shop floor — or a member of the board of directors. The 'user' may be an organisation or a group of people.

The user is anyone who has to use the system in any way. The user may be involved in many aspects of the system, or only a small part of it. A user may enter information into the system, or may only take information out of the system. Users may have jobs which are directed by the system, or may have a job that involves using the system to direct others. Some users have the task of controlling the system itself, by changing parameters, and deciding on and allowing access to various information or processes.

Users have widely differing characteristics which must be taken into consideration when an analyst is dealing with them. Users may be:

- well or poorly educated
- experienced or inexperienced
- old or young
- confident or timid
- helpful or unhelpful
- any other characteristic you can think of

Users may be egg-heads with Ph.D.s or technicians with professional and technical qualifications or experience. Users may be stalwart sergeants of the company who can remember 'the earlier, happier days' and who have a wealth of knowledge and understanding of the company and its activities. Such people, however, may never have been called upon to express or define this experience and knowledge. Users may be young school leavers with an uncaring attitude to their everyday work, or may be young school leavers with zeal, enthusiasm and a desire to rise rapidly through the company. Users may be of almost any level of education, intelligence, experience, responsibility or enthusiasm.

Understanding the User Environment

It is not possible for an analyst to produce and implement a design for new software systems or for changes to existing software systems without a thorough understanding of the organisation. It could be said that the techniques and tools of analysis are ways used by the analyst to understand the system. Many of the techniques in data analysis and data modelling are graphical. This is a relatively new concept and has arisen because of the need to communicate the understanding of the system to the user.

The business environment is a real, living, organism in the real world. Like any other system, it has inputs, outputs, stores and processes. The computer model of this environment can never be a perfect copy of the environment, and indeed may be an implementation of a part of the environment. It is important to realise that the environment can only be understood through the understanding of the human parts of that organisation - and that every human being in the organisation has a different view of the organisation. The function of the analyst is often to find a compromise between conflicting views of the same process or information structure.

The view of higher management is usually a general one, the view of operational staff is usually much narrower and specific. It is quite common for different departments or individuals to have conflicting aims and objectives and these must be resolved in any system which they all use.

The Business Analyst

The business analyst studies the organisation, records the understanding in the form of graphical images and uses these images to confirm understanding with the user. It is important not only that the systems or data designer understands the environment, but is seen by the users to understand it.

The job of the business analyst is to get from every single user their understanding of the organisation and its activities, its information needs and all the processes, inputs and outputs which are needed to do their particular job. For this reason, the best analysts are not just highly trained and knowledgeable about computers and computer systems, but are people who understand the nature of organisations and who have some understanding of how people tick.

The Hybrid Manager

This principle that computer professionals should have good business skills and knowledge if they are to become involved in analysing, specifying or supplying computer-based systems has been voiced in recent years by The British Computer Society. The BCS have advocated the concept of the hybrid manager.

A hybrid manager is a person who has training, skills and knowledge in both computing and business. Two ways have been suggested in which a person could become a hybrid manager. Firstly, such a person could be a computer professional who has cross-trained in business studies and who has gained experience in a business environment. Secondly, a hybrid manager could be a person who has training, skills and experience as a line manager in business and who has cross-trained in computer techniques and technology.

It is hoped that the increasing popularity of information systems as a subject of study and education may reduce the need for the idea of a hybrid. The word hybrid suggests a melding of two separate disciplines. It is better to accept that *information systems* is a discipline in its own right, bridging the gap between the business world and the world of the computer scientist.

In the same way that architects determine from their clients what kind of building is wanted, design it and supply the specifications to the building contractors, the information systems analyst determines from user organisations what is required and supplies specifications to the manufacturers of the hardware and software. The analogy is a very close one.

Understanding Expectations

Managing expectations is a subtle but very important part of the analyst's role in data modelling.

When the users are talking to an analyst about their job, their information needs and the way their job fits into the overall picture of the environment, they are perfectly aware that the objective, at the end of the day, will probably result in a new or changed computer system. They will have in their heads an expectation. This expectation may not be expressed — it may in fact be a vague and unstructured expectation which would be very difficult to express, even if they tried. Nevertheless, this expectation is there, and if the resulting system or database does not agree with this unspoken expectation, the user will be disappointed and will, to some degree or other, reject the new system or database.

It is vital for the analyst to be aware of these hidden expectations and to deal with them.

Managing Expectations

In order to avoid the disaster of the user saying 'But that's not at all what I wanted', the analyst must make an effort to clarify and adjust user expectations to match what is possible.

There was a case of a small software house which developed a system for an estate agent which would match up houses available on the books with enquiries from prospective buyers. The estate agent had asked for the system to be designed and built because the manual search of the paper database in the filing cabinets was taking hours for every enquiry. When the system was finished and installed the estate agent found that the computer search was taking ten, fifteen or even twenty minutes. The estate agent threw the system out and refused to pay for it, saying that he had been led to believe that the searches would be 'fast', by which he had understood a matter of seconds.

The process of analysis must be augmented with a touch of salesmanship, ensuring that the user has no unreasonable expectations of what the systems or the database will be able to do. Many people see computer systems as almost magical, and do not understand that machines are limited by technology, by what has been put in and by the fundamental design of the system itself.

It is a very good idea to produce a prototype of a system, so that you can show the user what they can expect. Users, as the saying goes, don't know what they want until they see what they don't want.

User Contact

Users are often, whether they admit it or not, afraid of change and of new technology. The analysts must build up a positive relationship with every user, but must make a particular effort to reassure those who are less flexible and who are apprehensive about new systems. Users have been known to be either deliberately or unconsciously obstructive or unhelpful when faced with an analyst. The user must understand that you are doing this to make their lives easier, not to make their job more complex or, even worse, to put them out of a job altogether.

Users may also be over-zealous. Users that have some knowledge of computing and who think that their own views are the right ones are very dangerous, especially if they are fairly senior or influential in the organisation. The analyst must build a good working relationship with the users and instil in them confidence that the design and implementation process is well-managed and in their interests.

User as Verifier of the Data Model

The techniques of data modelling should end up with an integrated, complete and consistent design for a database which is workable. In order to achieve this aim, the analyst must give feedback to the user on a regular basis, presenting the current state of the design in a professional and easy-to-understand way. Users will compare what they see presented by the analyst with their own knowledge and experience of their working environment. In this way the analyst will have the design confirmed.

It is important that the analyst does not blind the user with jargon or undue amounts of technical detail, otherwise the user will, quite rightly, complain that the analyst has not understood the environment. Worse still, the user may assume that his or her own understanding of what the analyst is showing them is lacking because of their own lack of knowledge of computing or data analysis. This will cause a breakdown in the relationship with the user and is inevitably the start of disaster. The user may well, in such a situation, say nothing. Silence is not assent when presenting a draft or complete data design to users. It is a very large red flag. Conversely, if the users volubly agree with your design, then you are getting somewhere and may well have cracked the basic understanding of their system.

Presentations to users must be

- paced right for the type of user
- clear
- pitched at the right detail level
- pitched at the right technical level

In one very large company, following the presentation of a very complex and detailed data model to the steering committee (composed of directors and senior managers) one director was heard to comment to the data analyst after the meeting: 'You know, in the thirty years I have been with this company, this is the first time I have really felt that I understand what we do'.

Information Gathering

The knowledge of the business environment from which the analyst constructs the data model does not come from thin air. There is really only one place to get this information and that is from the users — at every level and in every part of the organisation.

There are, however, some tried and tested ways of starting out. The environment, if it has been operating for some time, must have information systems already in place. This means that there will be existing stores of data and information and existing procedures for manipulating this information. Some of these stores and procedures may be computer-based, but many will not.

The analyst should ask users for a copy of all the paperwork which they use in their everyday work. You will not need a copy of every invoice or order, for example, but you will need copies of a few at least. The analyst should try to obtain copies of actual live documents, filled in or complete with the information held in the document. If there is a problem with security, which there may well be, the analyst can offer to erase the sensitive information from the copy. It is important, though, to establish the parameters of the information. How many lines in an address? How many characters are to be allowed for each line of the address? The length and type of each data item should be ascertained.

It is also important to stress to the user that the system will have to be able to deal with all cases, even the exceptional cases. The user may well tell you that, in the card index of customers, six lines are allowed for the address and may well show you examples of dozens of cards where six lines are not exceeded. At this point, the analyst should ask: what exceptions are there? When the user has shown you the few cards out of thousands where there are seven lines to the address, you should then ask: what are the other exceptions? The user will then — perhaps, if you are lucky — show you the one card, very old and well thumbed, of a customer in darkest Peru where there are nine lines on the card.

The analyst must dig — without appearing to pry or to be unduly harassing — in order to find the minimums and maximums which will support the system.

Once a copy of ordinary examples of every kind of document used in the environment has been obtained and recorded, a start has been made on the investigation of the data structure.

Be sure that there will be documentation and information which is a part of the system which is not unearthed by these investigations, but if the analyst continues to dig, to design and to feed back to the user the findings and the design, all should be revealed in the end.

Business Analysis

Summary

- Data modelling

  is a strategic business task
  is a result of communication between user and analyst
  must reflect user views
  must reflect management strategy for the business

- The business analyst

  has systems analysis and data analysis skills
  has business and organisational skills

CHAPTER 4

ENTITY RELATIONSHIP MODEL BASICS

☐ **What is an Entity Relationship Model? — Elements of the ERM — Types of entity — Attributes — Relationships between entities — Degree and membership — Relationship rules — Steps in ER modelling**

What is an Entity Relationship Model?

An Entity Relationship Model (ERM) is a logical (abstract) model of a set of entities and their relationships. Entity relationship modelling is used widely in industry as a part of the process of data design for databases. It is not normally used in isolation from other techniques and methods of data modelling, although it is taught and understood as a technique or method in its own right.

An entity, as will be explained in more detail very shortly, is something of interest about which we wish to store information, such as a car, a person, an invoice, a machine, a part or stock item.

An Entity Relationship Model (or ERM for short) is a diagram composed of rectangular boxes, representing entities, connected by lines, representing the relationships between the entities. The diagram is a simple and clear way of representing the analyst's understanding of the data structures being studied. The ERM is, however, much more than just a documentation tool. Because of its graphical nature, it is used by data analysts to communicate and confirm their understanding of the data structures with the users in the organisation. Although producing an ERM which can be transformed into a working and effective database is a long process, the ERM can be understood quite quickly. Within a few sessions, the users are able to explain and understand what the ERM is saying in terms of their own information environment.

Look at the diagram in Figure 4-1. This diagram is an ERM. In the diagram you will see four rectangular boxes, each uniquely and clearly labelled with a singular noun. Notice that the four boxes are all linked together to form a

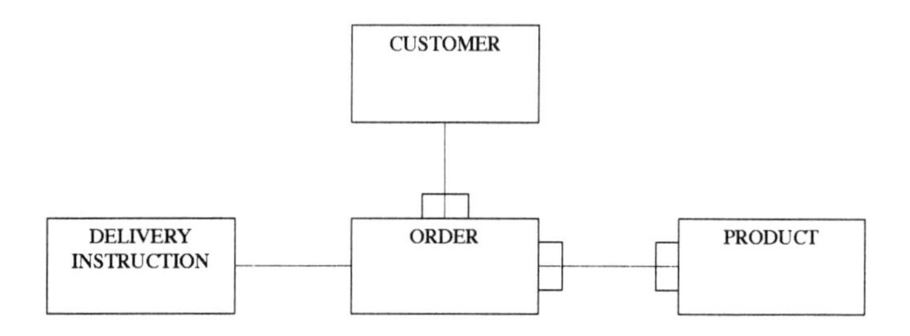

Figure 4-1 An Example of an ERM

single structure.

There are three relationship paths shown in the diagram, indicating the way that the entities relate to each other. Entities, their relationships and the exact meaning of the symbol conventions used will be examined in detail a little later on.

This diagram in Figure 4-1 makes the following statements:

> One order can have many products on it, and one product can appear on many orders.
>
> One delivery instruction can only appear on one order, and one order can only have one delivery instruction on it.
>
> One customer can have many orders, but one order can relate to only one customer.

As you will note, there is one statement (each composed of two discrete parts) for each of the relationship lines. These statements are called relationship rules, enterprise rules or business rules. In this case, some of these rules may not be true, either generally, or of a particular business operation, but the rules shown here reflect the diagram and the diagram is an expression of these rules. The relationship rule, then, is an English-like statement which is a direct and precise definition of the ERM relationship. If the rule were incorrect in the business context, then the ERM must be changed and the relationship rule will change accordingly.

Whether relationship rules are written and the ERM then drawn, or whether the ERM is drawn and the enterprise rules then written down is a matter of taste, style and approach, and both approaches are valid and may be mixed and matched. We will look at relationship rules and their syntax a little later on.

Elements of the ERM

One of the major advantages of the ERM as a diagrammatic tool in data modelling is its simplicity. Many diagramming techniques associated with computing or systems analysis have dozens of different symbols, making it very difficult to learn how to read such diagrams. The ERM contains only four symbol elements:

- rectangles representing entities
- connecting lines representing relationships
- tridents representing the degree of relationship
- dot markers representing the membership of relationships

Alternative Symbol Conventions

Although the entities are shown in the diagrams as rectangles, this is not the only symbol used in ER modelling. The rectangle is perhaps the most common conventional symbol, but others are used, such as an oval, or a hexagon. These symbols mean the same thing, but when drawing an ERM, data analysts must be consistent within the diagram and must adhere to the standards and conventions of the design environment within which they work. Similarly, the other elements of the ERM are drawn in different ways by people adhering to different conventions. In this book only one set of symbols will be used, for clarity, although alternatives may be mentioned for completeness. The kind of symbol used is irrelevant to the meaning of the ERM. Differences in symbol conventions are usually purely cosmetic.

We will now look at the meaning of each of these four conventional symbols in turn.

The Entity

What is an entity? An entity is a thing. The thing may be a physical object, such as a car, a building or a person. The thing may also be a logical or business object such as an invoice, an order or a job position. A thing may also be an event which occurs within an environment, such as a sale, a salary change or a business presentation. There exists within the ERM a fourth possible kind of entity, a link entity. This entity (of which we will hear more later) exists within the ERM and subsequently within the database because of the need to resolve special relationships in the ERM in order to fit the information structure into a relational database.

Types of Entity

While it is true to say that an entity is a thing, that may not seem very helpful at this stage. After all, everything is a thing, is it not?

There are several types of entities defined by those who study such things. An understanding of these distinctions between different types of entities is necessary for practical data modelling, and although we will not be delving into any of the theoretical aspects, we will look at some of these types in order to clarify the nature of an entity. Here are four types of entity:

- Physical entities
  Physical, or hard, entities can be touched and self-evidently exist in their own right. Such entities include people, physical objects or things such as motor vehicles, books or parcels. Some of these things will already have unique identifiers, but some will not, and have to have artificial identifiers attached to them.

- Logical entities
  Logical entities are recognised as having existence by the organisation and are a part of the organisation's operation. Examples of logical entities include orders, invoices and cheques. Be careful not to confuse the logical entity — for

example, a customer order — with a piece of paper on which the order might be recorded. Destroying the record of an order does not destroy the order itself, which is not physical, but logical.

- Event entities
  Event entities exist by virtue of having happened at a certain point in time. These are uniquely identified by a date-time stamp or an artificial code or number. A sale by a salesman, a repair carried out on a car, or a visit by a patient to a doctor are all event entities. These events are entities because they can be uniquely identified and because we wish to store information about the event.

- Link entities
  Link entities occur when the relationship between two other entities must be recorded separately from either entity. These are rather peculiar entities and will be considered in detail in a later chapter.

It is quite possible for an entity to belong to two or more of these types. An order, for example, is a logical entity (because it does not have a hard, physical existence) and an event entity (because an order was made by a customer at a certain point in time).

The definition of an entity for the purposes of ER modelling is that it has all three of the following characteristics:

- It has an independant existence and is capable of being uniquely identified
- It is the owner of attributes
- It is of interest to the enterprise or organisation

These three characteristics are essential for anything to be considered as an entity. If something cannot be uniquely identified, we cannot distinguish it from another of its kind and would be unable to retrieve any stored information about it. If it has no attributes — characteristics or owned information — there is no information about the thing to store in the first place. If it is of no interest to the organisation, we wouldn't want to store it anyway.

Continuous Entities

Caution should be used by the experienced data analyst in identifying entities and testing them against the three rules given in the last section. Not all things which must be handled as entities for the purposes of data modelling satisfy these rules.

In a data analysis and design exercise for a major chemical company, the analysts concerned were faced with the problem of tracking, using a computer database, quantities of chemicals of all kinds through a chemical processing plant. For want of a better term, some entities are continuous, rather than discrete.

There are many cases of quantities of substances being handled in computer databases. Examples include volumes of flour, yeast or caramel in a bakery, volumes of milk and milk-products in many different states in a dairy, petroleum products in various states in a refinery or quantities of various seeds in a wholesale garden centre.

Some items, while discrete, are not uniquely identified, and are treated as a volume, such as washers, nails, nuts and bolts. Many of these substances may be enclosed in packages, sacks or drums, which may be uniquely identifiable. Referring to the containers may be the only way of tracking the substances as entities. This may, however, present other difficulties. In the chemical plant referred to above, chemicals were drained or pumped from tank to tank, mixed in mixing tanks and would often produce a resultant liquid — or even a solid — with an entirely different chemical name and with quite different properties. The resultant of mixing two volumes did not necessarily have the same volume as the two constituent substances added together. One of the requirements of the system was to measure and attempt to reduce wastage.

This particular problem was solved by identifying batches of liquid or solid by date and time of filling and location within a numbered tank. Other solutions might have worked equally well, but this example is given to demonstrate to the reader that neither things nor entities are always as straightforward as one might wish.

Unique Identifier

A car or house has a unique identity. A car has a registration number, and if not registered can be identified by a chassis number. Both registration numbers and chassis numbers are unique identifiers of car. A house has a unique address, certainly when the post code is included. An order or invoice is uniquely identified by a number given to it by the organisation when it comes into existence. Identifying an event entity such as a salary change or sale is a little more problematical and would probably involve a combination of a date-time stamp, who was involved and where the event occurred. Often, though, events are given unique numbers or codes by the organisation.

The advent of the information age and the widespread use of computer technology has meant that most things in the world of interest now have unique identifiers. The unique identifier of a person, arguably, is their genetic code plus their life history, but this cannot be stored effectively in a computer. So we use artificial numbers instead, like a National Health Service number or a National Insurance number. Care must be taken when considering the unique identifier of an entity. Although a data analyst might be tempted to use the National Insurance number as a unique identifier, in a hospital or school environment this wouldn't work: children don't have National Insurance numbers.

Although many things are self-evidently entities, unique and with their own identity, very few have natural unique identifiers by which we can identify them. A driving licence number does not uniquely identify a person, but identifies the logical entity of the person's right to drive a car.

The unique identifier is required by the relational model, and must be present in the tables for an entity in a relational database. Unique identification is not so essential for object oriented databases, but is often present whether the data analyst needs it or not. The unique identifier is often called a primary key. Any item of information or combination of items which can be chosen as the unique identifier of an entity is known as a candidate key. Some entities may have more than one candidate key. For example, a car, depending on the nature of the information system and why the information is being stored, might be uniquely identified by the registration number or the chassis number.

Attributes

All entities have attributes or characteristics. Attributes are often analogous to adjectives, which describe a noun. A car has a colour and an engine capacity. A house has a number of rooms and a number (possibly zero) of garages. Orders and invoices have dates, customers and a sum of money. A sale has a salesman, a customer and a value. A salary increase has a person, a percentage increase value and a date. Evidently, these entities are of interest to some organisation or enterprise because of the organisation's interest in recording the attributes.

The attributes of a thing can be thought of in the same way as the columns in a table where a line of the table relates to one occurrence of the entity. In the table below, the attributes of a person are shown.

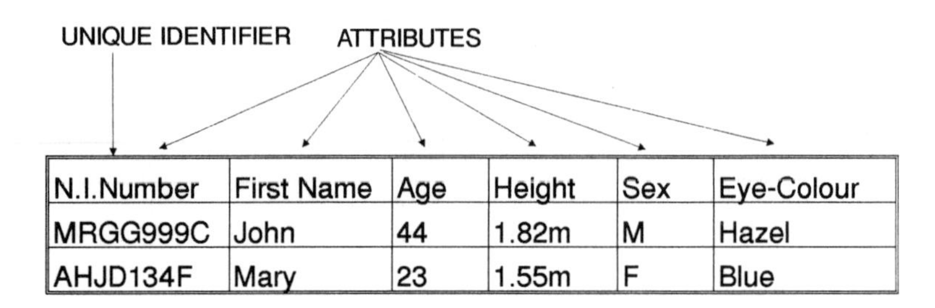

N.I.Number	First Name	Age	Height	Sex	Eye-Colour
MRGG999C	John	44	1.82m	M	Hazel
AHJD134F	Mary	23	1.55m	F	Blue

Figure 4-2 Examples of Attributes of Entity

The entity person has the attributes NI Number, Name, Age, Height, Sex and Eyes, amongst others.

The unique identifier is also an attribute of an entity because it is an item of information belonging to that entity.

It is clearly the case that the attributes of some things are almost unlimited. It is impossible, for example, to record all the attributes of a person — every characteristic, quality and item of information which belongs to that person. The only true definition of the thing is the thing itself. For the purposes of data modelling, however, we only record those attributes which we need to store. Each organisation which wants to store information about a thing will be interested in different characteristics.

What information might we want to store about a motor car or vehicle, for example?

- Ford Motor Cars
  Ford might well want to keep details of every last assembly, part, nut and bolt, the specification of the steel in every panel, the mathematical definition of the curves of the body, and much, much more.
- The police
  Because they need the information for different purposes, the police might require the registration number of the car, the

owner's name, the date of registration, make and model, colour, engine capacity, and any history of the car changing hands or being involved in nefarious events.

In a later chapter, we will look at cases where attributes can, in certain circumstances, be viewed as entities in their own right. But for the moment, let us view them simply as bits of information about an entity.

Relationships

The relationship between two entities can be seen simply as ownership or as a kind of parent-child relationship. In Figure 4-1, these relationships could be described in terms of either ownership or as a parent-child relationship.

```
One order may own or possess many products.

One product can be owned by many orders.

One customer can be the parent of many orders.

One order is the child of only one customer.
```

Relationships can also be viewed as the verbs or actions by which entities relate to each other.

```
A customer may place many orders but an order
must be placed by one and only one customer.

An order may be placed for many products and a
given product may be ordered on many orders.
```

The nature of the relationship between two entities will become clearer as the details of ERMs are explored.

Degree of Relationship Symbols

Any two entities which have a relationship will have one of only three degrees or types of relationship.

- One-to-one
- One-to-many
- Many-to-many

These three degrees or types of relationship are the only possible and one of them must apply. A one-to-one relationship exists between husband and wife (at least in the culture I belong to) because a wife can have only one husband and a husband can have only one wife. (See Figure 4-3.)

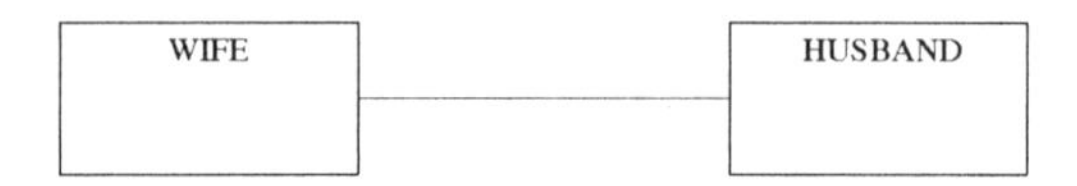

Figure 4-3 One-To-One Relationship

A wife has one husband and a husband has one wife.

The relationship between natural mother and daughter is one-to-many because a mother may have (own or be the parent of) many daughters, but a daughter can have only one natural mother. (See Figure 4-4.)

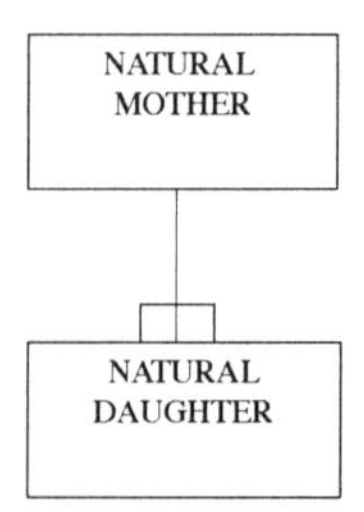

Figure 4-4 One-To-Many Relationship

A natural mother may have one or many natural daughters, but a natural daughter has one and only one natural mother.

An example of a many-to-many relationship is between a customer order and a product, because an order may relate to many products (may have many products on it) and a product may appear on or relate to many orders. (See Figure 4-5.)

The many-to-many relationship is a special case, because it cannot be stored or represented in a database without special steps being taken. Solving a

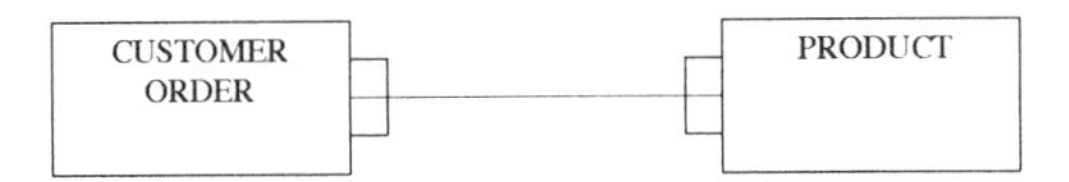

Figure 4-5 Many-To-Many Relationship

A Customer Order may include many products and a product may appear on many Customer Orders.

many-to-many involves using a link entity, which we saw earlier in this chapter. This will be dealt with in detail in a later chapter.

In the figures illustrating the three types of degree of relationship, you will notice the convention for *many* is a trident, used because it indicates *many* links to the entity as opposed to the *one* end of the relationship line. The trident is only a convention and other symbols are used as well, including single and double arrows, a semicircle or a crow's foot (See Figure 4-6.)

All of these conventional symbols mean the same thing, but when using these symbols on an ERM it is important firstly to be consistent and secondly to adhere to the conventions in use in the department or environment in which the ERM is being developed. Perhaps the most important factor in deciding which symbol to use is the user's preference. If the user has seen ERMs before, it will be easier to understand the familiar symbol. Most data analysts stick to the conventions that they were trained to use and change only with effort. The purpose of the ERM is communication, and the conventions which communicate most clearly to the user and the analyst are the best.

Membership Markers

The fourth conventional symbol which appears on an ERM is the membership marker. This is a dot placed at the end of the relationship line. If the relationship is mandatory, that is the entity must take part in the relationship, a dot is placed inside the entity rectangle. If the relationship is optional, the dot is placed outside the entity rectangle, on the relationship line. This dot or marker shows whether or not the two entities must have a relationship, or whether the relationship is optional.

Sometimes the terms *obligatory* and *non-obligatory* are used instead of *mandatory* and *optional*, but the sense is the same. In the case of the husband

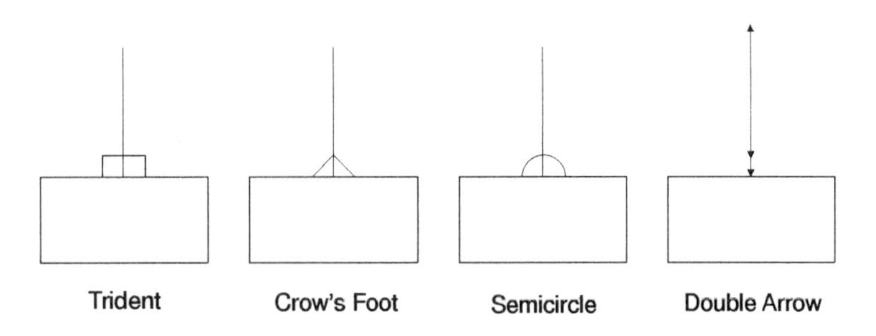

Figure 4-6 Various 'Many' Symbol Conventions

There is no difference in the semantics (meaning) of these various symbols. They are all used in different environments.

and wife, the relationship is mandatory for both the entities, for the simple reason that a husband is not a husband and the wife is not a wife if the relationship does not exist. Another example of membership might be that of a commercial aircraft flight and a pilot. A pilot can exist without a flight (the pilot may just have been entered onto the database and has not been on a flight yet) but a flight could surely not exist without a pilot. (See Figure 4-7.)

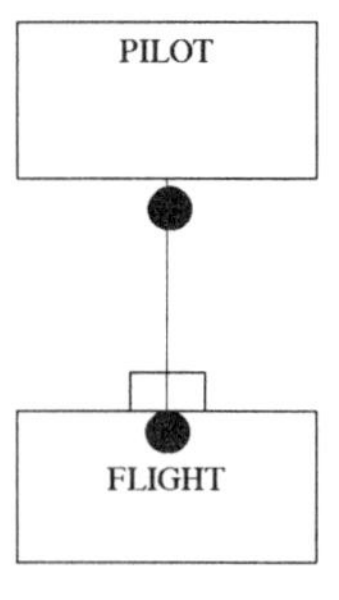

Figure 4-7 Examples of Membership Marking

The dot markers indicate that the flight cannot exist without a pilot, but that a pilot can exist without a flight.

Generally, relationships mostly fall into the natural relational pattern of the owning or parent entity having optional membership (the parent does not have to have a child) but the owned or child entity having a mandatory relationship with its parent (a child must have a parent).

Figure 4-7 illustrates the use of membership markers. It must be clearly understood that, like in a genealogical chart, any entity can be both a parent and a child at the same time.

Relationship Rules

As has been said, a *relationship rule* is an English-like statement which expresses the semantic meaning of the relationship in an ERM. It is an extremely useful element of the data modelling process and the designer of an ERM should always state the enterprise rule for a relationship, either in writing or verbally, to allow thinking and common sense to detect the truth or falsehood (sometimes absurdity) of the assertion being made.

The syntax of the enterprise rule is not thought to be very strict in some circles of data modelling, but a possible, general syntax for the relationship rule is given here for clarity. Not all enterprise rules will adhere to this syntax, but if the designer follows this syntax in most cases, the semantics of the enterprise rule may well be improved.

```
A [first entity] may/must [relation verb] zero,
one or many [second entity] and a [second
entity] may/must [relation verb] zero, one or
many [first entity]
```

In the above syntax the word *may* should be replaced with the word *must* for clarity when zero is not an option (i.e. when the relationship line is mandatory for the entity).

The *relation verb* should be a verb of possession, parenthood or relation which makes the English sentence clear and informative.

The *zero, one or many* phrase should be used appropriately. The various options for this specification of the degree of the relationship are :

- zero, one or many
- zero or one
- one

- one or many

For even greater clarity, the third option *one* could be written as *one and only one*. Both this and the general syntax of the enterprise rule described contain redundancy, but redundancy is very useful where human understanding is concerned.

The previous paragraphs may seem a little technical to some (although there will be technical computer people who think the converse). A number of examples of the structure and use of enterprise rules are given in Figure 4-8.

```
An order may have zero, one or many
order-lines, but an order-line must
relate to one and only one order.

A patient may have many treatments,
but a treatment must relate to one
and only one patient.

Over a period of time a driver may
drive zero, one or many cars and a
given car may be driven by zero, one
or many drivers.
```

Figure 4-8 Examples of Relationship Rules

The relationship rules are structured statements about the relationship between two entities.

Steps in ER Modelling

While there is no hard and fast method or methodology in creating an ERM, a data analyst will always pass through a number of steps, tasks or processes before arriving at a first draft ERM. These steps or tasks might include the following:

- investigate the environment
- identify the entities
- establish the relationship between the entities

- determine the degree of each relationship
- solve all many to many relationships and any other connection problems
- write the enterprise rules
- verify the ERM and the enterprise rules with the user

This list of steps is not definitive and it is not a formal method or methodology. In a later chapter we will be looking in more detail at the way a development team will approach the creation of a design for a database, within the context of systems development.

Many of these steps will happen in parallel and an ERM may often never show any many-to-many relationships or traps because the designer has thoroughly understood the nature of the business environment and the relational model and has automatically or intuitively eliminated them before formally putting pencil to paper.

Other Data Modelling Tools

Entity relationship modelling will very rarely succeed in producing a workable model of a real world information environment without using other tools in conjunction with entity modelling.

Normalisation, Data Flow Diagrams and Entity Life History diagrams are topics which exist in their own right and are covered separately in later chapters. It must be stressed that all these techniques operate in conjunction and are far less beneficial in isolation. Producing an ERM without applying an understanding of normalisation of data is like trying to ride a bicycle with only one wheel. Some people are good at it, but they are normally found in circuses, not in information systems environments.

Soft Technique

There is no such thing as a correct ERM. Every source of information from which we obtain information about the information environment will see the environment from a subtly different point of view. These subtle (and sometimes not so subtle) differences have to be resolved by the analyst. The resultant ERM must be acceptable to all those who will use the database or system, but will differ slightly from some of the user views. Furthermore, very few, if any, organisations or information structures are static and the ERM which represents the changing environment should change too.

The more dynamic an organisation is, the faster the ERM will become obsolete. An ERM must be seen as a snapshot of a compromise. ERMs are not right or wrong, they are workable or unworkable when they have been translated into a database structure.

The process of data modelling in a business environment can and does highlight situations where the working practices of the business or enterprise could be changed for the better. It is important that the designer models the system for the user. The question of there being a difference between what the user says he needs and what the designer thinks he needs is a very difficult one. Should the designer bow to the user's wishes even though he feels sure that the design the user wants is not the best? This dilemma faces all professionals at one time or another, and the answer to the question will depend on the designer's ethics.

Logical not Physical

The process of ER modelling has nothing to do with computer files. Many experienced computer professionals make the mistake of thinking of entities as being computer files and are immediately trapped into physical thinking. This is usually disastrous. Physical thinking means considering the implementation of these objects on a computer. This is not appropriate when modelling data structures in a real-world information system.

We are studying the information structures of an environment when designing an ERM, and considering the things in that environment and their relationships. We are not talking about a database or file structure, at least not yet. The ERM, when complete and verified, may indeed be translated into the form of a set of relational tables which may in turn be implemented as files in a computer file system or a relational database management system (RDBMS), but this happens later.

Techniques Work Together

The basic concepts that have been explained in this chapter are fundamental to an understanding of data modelling. They will become clearer and more natural to the designer after the other aspects of modelling, to be found in later chapters, have been understood. The statement made earlier, that data modelling is a skill which uses several techniques, means that it is more difficult to understand as a skill when only one technique has been understood. After reading and understanding the chapters which cover normalisation, entity connections and traps, Data Flow Diagrams, the Logical Data

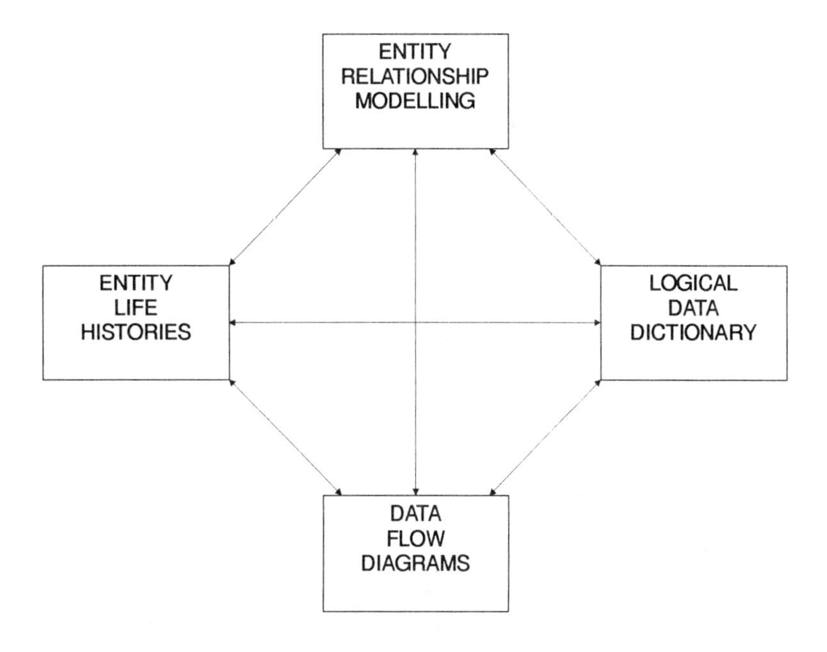

Figure 4-9 Data Modelling

This diagram shows how data modelling is a complex combination of a number of different techniques: ER modelling, Entity Life Histories, Logical Data Dictionary and Data Flow Diagrams.

Dictionary and Entity Life History diagrams, the techniques will blend into an understanding of the data model as a whole. (See Figure 4-9.) The data model is not the diagram, nor any collection of diagrams, but the model in the mind of the designer — and the user — as expressed by the diagrams.

Entity Relationship Model Basics

Summary

- An ERM is a diagram showing the data analyst's understanding of a real-world information environment. It is composed of

  entity rectangles

  relationship lines

  degree of relationship symbols

  membership markers

- The ERM is used to

  record the analyst's understanding

  impose a formal approach to data design

  communicate and confirm understanding with the user community

  provide a discussion and brainstorming tool when discussing the information structures

- Relationship rules reiterate the meaning of the relationship lines in the ERM in a structured English-like way to allow confirmation of the correctness of the relationship line's meaning.
- An entity is a thing. For the purpose of the ERM an entity must

  be capable of being uniquely identified

  be the owner of attributes or characteristics

  be of interest to the organisation concerned

- An attribute is a discrete item of information about an entity.
- There are only three kinds of relationship in an ERM

  one-to-one

  one-to-many

  many-to-many

- There are only four kinds of membership of a relationship by an entity zero, one or many

zero or one

one

one or many

- If zero is one of the possibilities, then the relationship is optional — otherwise, it is mandatory.

CHAPTER 5

ENTITY RELATIONSHIP MODELLING CONNECTIONS

☐ **ERM Connections — Resolving Many-To-Many Relationships — Connection Traps — Fan Traps — Chasm Traps — Bypass and Override Solutions**

Entity Relationship Model Connections

Once the Entity Relationship Model has been started, showing the entity boxes and their relationships, it is necessary to take the design a step further. So far, we have inserted the one-to-one, one-to-many and many-to-many relationships which we have been able to identify. We must now look at these in more detail, starting with the many-to-many relationships.

Resolving Many-To-Many Relationships

Many-to-many relationships cannot be supported by a relational model or an RDBMS. The reason for this is that if we implement the entities which form a many-to-many relationship as tables in a relational environment it is impossible to tell which occurrences of either table relate to the occurrences of the other table. In the case of one-to-one or one-to-many where at least one of the entities has a compulsory relationship, the ownership of one entity of another is embedded as an identifier in the owned entity. In the case of a many-to-many, usually neither entity has a compulsory relationship with the other and the data relationship between the two entities cannot be determined. In this case a link entity must be created to hold the detail of the relationship between the two.

Figure 5-1 Many-To-Many must be resolved

The relationship rule for this ERM is: Entity A may be associated with many Entity B, and Entity B may be associated with many Entity A.

From an ERM point of view this is done by creating a new entity , the link entity, often named by both its owning entities hyphenated, and reversing the degree of the relationship. (See Figures 5-1 and 5-2.)

The link entity holds the occurrences of the relationship between the two entities it links.

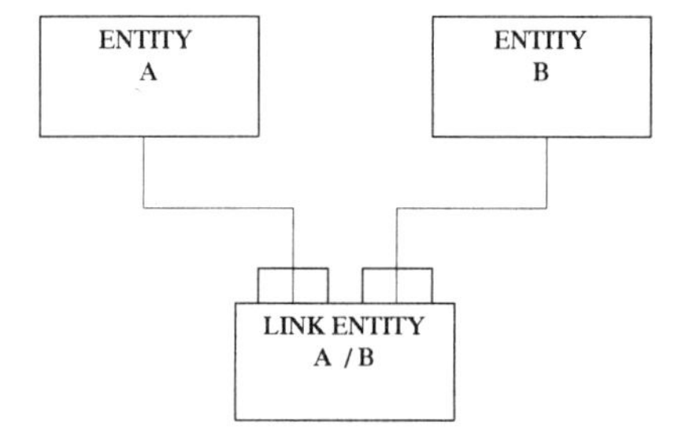

Figure 5-2 Many-To-Many resolved

The Many-to-Many has been solved, and the Link entity A/B will now contain an entry for every case of A and B relating.

In Figure 5-3, the tables *car* and *driver* are shown, with a few of their many possible attributes. In the link table *driven*, the unique identifiers of both *car* and *driver* appear. In effect, this table records the instances of the relationship between *car* and *driver* — in this case, the period of time during which the driver was associated with the car. Great care must be taken to see the principle behind this example. There are numerous many-to-many relationships in any ERM of any complexity, and they must be recognised and dealt with by the designer. This one is just an example. There are a further couple of points of interest; one of the *end-date* attribute cells is empty in the table

Car		
Registration	Make	CC
A123XYZ	Ford	1300
POW456T	Mazda	1600

Driver		
Driver-No	Surname	DOB
JON1235	Jones	12.1.55
SMI5434	Smith	1.5.62

Driven			
Registration	Driver-No	Start-Date	End-Date
A123XYZ	JON1235	17.7.88	21.3.90
A123XYZ	SMI5434	22.3.90	25.6.90
POW456T	SMI5434	13.6.91	29.7.91
POW456T	JON1235	7.12.90	
GHI 98 X	BRO5432	8.11.91	9.7.92
G 111SSD	BRO5432	7.6.90	9.6.90

Figure 5-3 Tables Illustrating The Link Entity

Car and Driver have a Many-To-Many relationship. The Link entity Driven contains the occurrences of the relationship between Car and Driver.

driven. This is deliberate, because it shows that the car is still being driven — that the period has not ended. There is a question as to whether the data is missing, and whether or not we have wasted space here in conflict with the aims of data modelling — these issues will be addressed in a later chapter.

With the addition of this link entity, the problem is now solved and the model, although slightly less simple and elegant, is able to fully support the enterprise's needs. In the example shown, cars have their own unique identifier, registration number. Cars have many drivers associated with them. Drivers, too, have a unique identifier; driving licence number. Drivers are associated with many cars. (Remember that we are referring to a particular set of rules for one organisation — these statements need not be true of every environment involving cars and drivers.) The table *car* cannot have driver references inserted into it: how many drivers do we have? It could be thousands. Nor can the table *driver* have the identifier for cars inserted into it — for the same reason. We solve the problem by creating another entity — a link entity — to hold the relationship between *car and driver.*

Connection Traps

There are a number of possible problems when drawing an ERM, which result in a failure of the model to establish a relationship between two entities which need to be linked to provide information neccessary to fulfil the enterprise's needs. Two of these problems have a very distinctive pattern in the ERM and have been given their own names (Howe 1983). These two traps are called:

- fan traps
- chasm traps

Fan Traps

Fan traps take their name from the shape or appearance of the entity occurrence diagram (see Figure 5-6) . These traps are found in situations where there is a M:1-1:M pattern between three entities and where the two entities separated from each other by the central entity do in fact have a logical relationship. In Figure 5-4 you will see that the pattern of the relationships shows that a division has many branches and a division has many staff. Staff and branches both relate to only one division.

While these statements are true, and while the enterprise rules built from the diagram would be correct, the ERM and the enterprise rules fail to show that

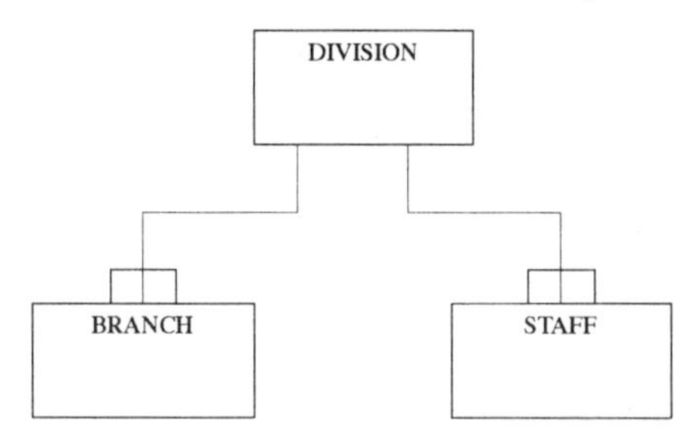

Figure 5-4 Fan Trap

A Division relates to many Branches and to many Staff. How do we know which Branch a member of Staff works for? Do we need to know?

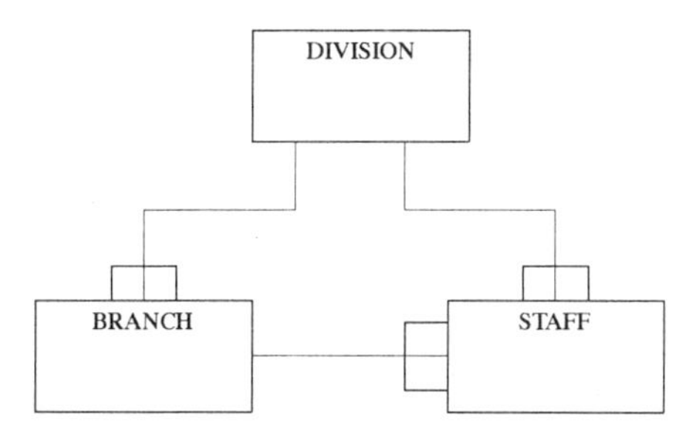

Figure 5-5 Fan Trap Solved?

We have marked the relationship between Branch and Staff. Have we solved the problem, or not?

staff relate to one branch and that a branch has many staff. Because of the missing relationship between branch and staff, it is impossible to determine which staff relate to which branches. The model is incomplete and will fail to fulfil the enterprise's needs. The gap between branch and staff cannot be bridged unless the model is changed. The most obvious way of curing the problem is to create a new relationship between branch and staff (see Figure 5-5). This, however, can lead to another possible trap, the chasm trap.

It is important to stress that the assumptions made about the business in the previous paragraph are given to illustrate the description of a fan trap. The question, in real life, which must be asked about a potential fan trap pattern

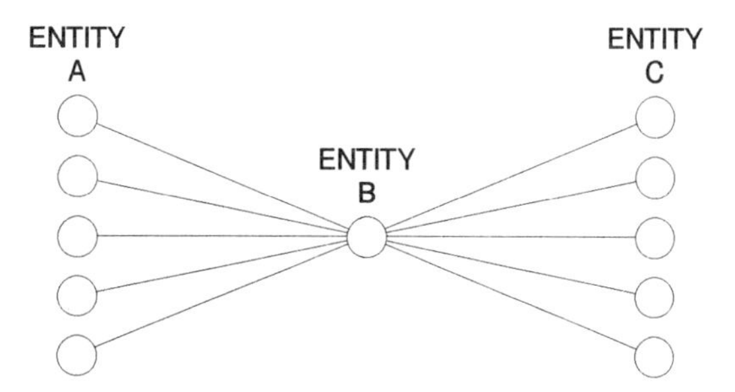

Figure 5-6 Entity Occurrence Diagram For The Fan Trap

For each occurrence of entity B, there are a number of occurrences of both entity A and entity C. The question must be asked: Do entity A and entity C relate directly?

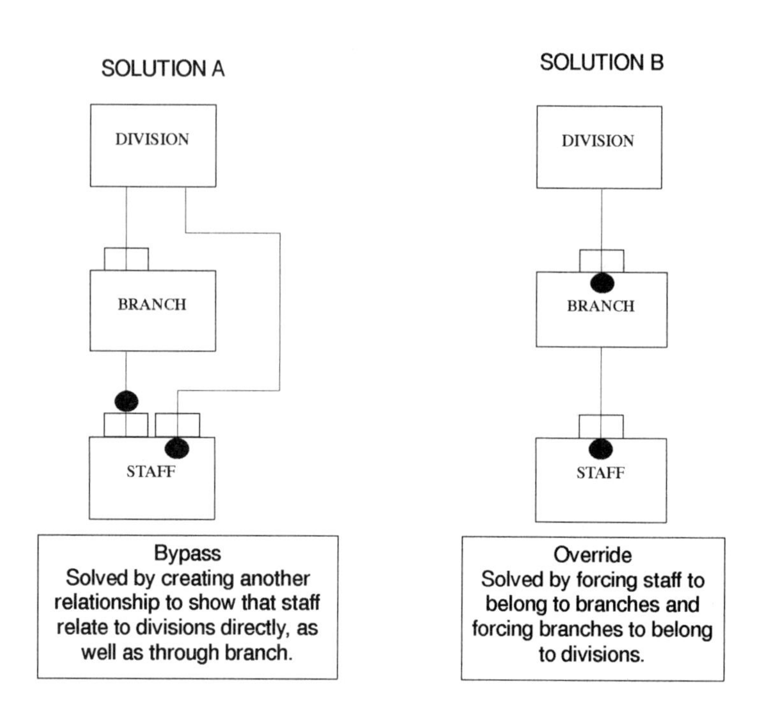

Figure 5-7 The Two Solutions to the Chasm Trap

Staff always belong to a Division, but do not necessarily belong to a Branch. How, then, can we be sure of knowing to which Division a member of Staff belongs?

(M:1-1:M) is: 'Does the business need to know about any relationship between the entities on either side of the fan?' If there is no relationship, then the trap does not exist. If there is a relationship, the trap exists and must be solved.

Chasm Traps

The chasm trap is a close relative of the fan trap and often follows on from it. In Figure 5-5, you will see that we have solved the division-staff-branch fan trap by inserting a relationship between staff and branch. It naturally follows that we assume that we can now remove the path between division and staff, since the ownership of staff by division is now shown through branch. We know which branch each member of staff belongs to through the staff-branch relationship and we know which division each branch belongs to through the division-branch relationship. It therefore follows that we can determine which staff work for which division by following these two paths. The link between division and staff is therefore redundant. Or is it?

The question which must be asked at this point is 'is every member of staff part of a branch?' If there is a case of a member of staff who is not a member of a branch (such as a divisional director) then the link through *branch* is lost and we can no longer determine which *division* that member of staff works for. If the relationship between *staff* and *branch* is optional at both ends then a chasm trap exists, and must be solved.

There are two ways to resolve a chasm trap. The first is mainly for the purist and the second is mainly for the pragmatist. Both are effective and choosing between them is a matter of weighing the circumstances and the enterprise's view (as expressed by the users).

Bypass Solution

The first way is to retain the relationship between *division* and *staff* to cater for the exceptions to the rule that staff belong to branches. (See Figure 5-7(A).) For those staff who do not belong to branches we can now determine to which division they belong.

The disadvantages of this way of resolving the trap are, firstly, that it creates more complexity in the ERM. It is rarely the case that complexity is desirable and it is far more often the case that the simpler the ERM is the better. The second reason is that an overhead has been created for indexing purposes (or for whatever method is used by the file system or the RDBMS to maintain the new link). Whether this overhead is significant and should be avoided depends on the volumes of the data in the various datasets and the opinion of the Database Administrator (DBA).

Override Solution

The second way of resolving the chasm trap is to insert a dummy occurrence in the Branch entity to allow the linkage though the entity to occur. (See Figure 5-7(B).) At the same time, in order to enforce this method of resolution, the membership of the relationship by the owning entity must be made mandatory.

In the case of the divisional director, this would mean having an entry in the branch entity such as 'dummy' or 'divisional staff'. Although this is strictly distorting the natural data of the enterprise (there simply isn't a branch called dummy in the organisation) it does have the advantage of simplicity. There are no overheads of maintaining a second index, no triggers or extra rules in the database processing and the meaning of the branch name is explicit. There is a case for arguing that there is indeed a logical branch called 'divisional staff', even though the organisation does not recognise it.

Entity Relationship Model Connections

Summary

- The existence of a many-to-many relationship in an ERM is not supportable by the relational model. Many-to-many relationships must be resolved by creating a link entity between the two entities to store the detail of their relationship. The M:M relationship becomes a 1:M - M:1 (degree is reversed)

- A Fan Trap exists when

  three entities form a M:1 - 1:M pattern

  and

  the two outer entities have a relationship

- If no relationship exists between the two outer entities, no Fan Trap exists.

- A Fan Trap is resolved by inserting the relationship line between the related entities.

- A Chasm Trap exists where access to a relationship between two entities through a third may be broken by the absence of the intermediate entity occurrence.

- A Chasm Trap is resolved

  by bypassing the intermediate entity and retaining the relationship line between the two related entities which are separated by the intermediate entity

  OR

  by overriding the optionality of the relationship, thus forcing the existence of the entity occurrence in the intermediate entity and using a dummy occurrence (or record).

CHAPTER 6

FIVE-A-SIDE FOOTBALL LEAGUE

This chapter takes the form of a case study, to allow the ideas, concepts and techniques discussed up to this point to be seen in action. In this chapter, we will see a simple requirement for a database examined by a data analyst, and see how the analyst, by talking to the user and refining the design, reaches an elegant, workable solution to the user's problem.

This case study is developed from a fraction of the information which would be available in the real world. It is important to remember that no real life situation would be as straight forward as this scenario, designed to illustrate the principles of data modelling so far described in this book. Nor will the reader find that the scenario necessarily agrees completely with their real-world experience of football or sports leagues. There are also a number of particularly elegant aspects to this case study which might not appear in a less elegant, but just as workable, solution to similar problems in the real world.

General Information

Harry Jones is nearing retirement, and chaos may soon ensue. For many, many years, Harry has been the keeper of the records for the Five-A-Side Football League. He is very proud of his system, which is kept meticulously on index cards. He explains that he is able to find out who played, who scored and when the goal was scored, for any game played in the last 25 years.

The league, however, has discovered that no-one can understand Harry's system. The index cards for the team and the fixture (see Figures 6-5 and 6-6 at the end of this case study) have been supplied by Harry. Harry explains the cards:

> Each team card has the name, address and telephone number of the team manager, and the team's name. It also has a list of all the players registered for that club. The name and address of the team coaches are also present, with their telephone number if we need to contact them. The manager or the coach contacts the club's own members.
>
> Teams meet whenever they want for training, but fixtures are nearly always played on a Sunday afternoon or a Wednesday evening.
>
> The second card, the fixtures card (Figure 6-6), also contains a lot of information. This card shows the names of both teams playing at the fixture, the first team being the home team. The date and venue of the fixture are given, the score at the end of the game, and a list of the players who actually played in the match. Next to each player's name is a number, which is the minute in which that player scored a goal. On the card shown, Baldwyn, Oldham and Rudgely have each scored one goal, but it is possible — even likely, that some players will score two or more goals. In this case, two numbers would appear next to the player's name.

Harry also points out that the referee's name and address appear on this card, although he agrees that there is a great deal of duplication, and that often he doesn't write in the address, to save writing it too often. There are only a few referees and he usually looks through the cards until he finds a card with the referee's address shown. He has been thinking about creating an index of referees, but so far hasn't needed to.

As well as talking to Harry, and obtaining copies of the cards he uses, we have also talked to the league secretary. The league's secretary explains that there a number of outputs required from the system. These are:

- The league table
  The league table is a list of teams ranked according to points gained during games. The number of games won, drawn or lost is included in this list.

- The membership list
  This is simply an alphabetical list of members of the league, showing the member's details including the team they belong to. Harry thinks it would be interesting to show the number of hat-tricks scored by the player in the last 3 seasons, but when he sees the expression on the analyst's face, admits that this particular requirement can wait.

- The game report
  The game report is a statement of a game on a date and is to include the date, time and venue, the teams playing, the names of the scoring players and the minutes in which they scored the goal.

Although other information may well be required in future, the league secretary does not require any other outputs at this time. We now have some basic information about what is required as information from the new system, and by implication, the information which will need to be input to allow the required information to be produced.

This information is obviously very sketchy, but for the purposes of the case study it is sufficient to show how we get from the initial requirements to a working model.

Discussion

First of all, let us start with the analysis of the two index cards which Harry has supplied. The first card, the team card, contains a number of clear entities. (See Figure 6-5.)

A *team* is a discrete thing, identifiable and different from other teams. It has characteristics: its name, its players and its playing colours, its date of formation and its position in the league. It is definitely of interest to the league. It is a very strong candidate for an entity. We could now produce a table of attributes for this entity. The table of attributes has the name of the entity first, followed in brackets by a list of its attributes. The first attribute is the unique identifier or primary key and is underlined. What might the table for *team* look like?

Team(Team-Name, Team-Manager, Team-Coach,
Team-Colours, Date-Formed, League-Position)

Where will the information about the manager and coach go? Could these go in this table?

> Team(<u>Team-Name</u>,Team-Manager, Manager-Address, Manager-Telephone,Team-Coach,Coach-Address, Coach-Telephone, Team-Colours, Date-Formed, League-Position)

Player is a clear entity, all people are physical entities. Is there a relationship between *team* and *player*? Yes, there is. A team has many players and a player plays for one team. Harry confirms that this is so. Harry agrees with the rule for this relationship.

```
A team may have zero,one or many players, but
a player must belong to one and only one team.
```

We have made a start on the ERM (see Figure 6-1). What might the table for the entity *player* look like? (Remember that we are only, as yet, exploring this model — any tables we envisage at this stage may well change before we have finalised the model.)

> Player(<u>Registration-Number</u>, Player-Surname, Player-Initials, Player-Date-Of-Birth, Player-Address, Player-Telephone)

What is the difference between a player and a coach or a manager? Certainly the player plays in games, where the coach or manager don't — or do they?

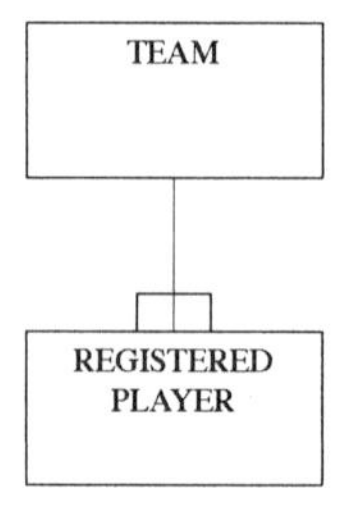

Figure 6-1 Five-A-Side ERM: A Team Has Many Players

The rule for this small ERM is: a team may have zero, one or many players, but a player must belong to one and only one team.

'Oh, no', says Harry, 'managers and coaches are often players!'

Hold on. What information do we need to hold about people? Name, address and telephone number, in every case. The attributes of *player* and of *manager* and *coach* are the same. So why store them in different tables? Why not use another attribute, called, say, *member-type*? This would hold the information as to what kind of member the person is: player, manager or coach. This may be very problematical.

What if a member is manager and coach for a team and plays as well? Can a member be coach for two different teams? If the answer to these questions were affirmative, it would make the model very much more complicated, to represent all roles. Let us revert, partly, to our previous solution. Let us keep the reference to the manager and the coach in the *team* table. This appears to be the simplest solution to the problem at the moment, although we may come back to it later.

On the fixture card (see Figure 6-6) we find a list of the five players who played at the fixture. This is, presumably, a subset of the registered players. Harry isn't sure about this. Can a player play on the day without being a registered player? Yes. How then will we enter this person to the system without a registration number? 'I don't know about registration numbers,' says Harry. 'We have never had them before, why do we need them?'

'We need to have a number because the computer needs it. The computer would not be able to identify two different people who happen to have the same name. It is easier to use a number. When someone plays who isn't registered, you will give them a special number starting with a '9'. We will give you a clear set of instructions on how to deal with this problem.'

Harry shakes his head sadly and expresses thanks that he will be retiring soon.

Those who play games such as five-a-side football may be tempted to ask the question: is there a difference between team and club? Does, for example, any club have more than one team? In the interests of keeping this case study relatively simple, let us say that we have asked Harry and that he has assured the analyst that no club has more than one team, and will not have more than one team in the future.

There is also the entity *venue* on the second card. It is of interest, it is unique and identifiable, and it has attributes. The *game* itself is also an entity. A *game* can be played at only one venue, but a venue may have many games played at it. It is also true that a game is associated with many goals, but that a goal must be associated with one and only one game. Remember though that this is only an early draft ERM, and that the relationship between *game* and *goal* may lie elsewhere. *Goal* has the player (who scored it) as one of its attributes. This establishes the link with *player*.

Let's have a look at Figure 6-2 for a moment. There is no link between *player* and *game*, yet. There definitely is a link in real life. The fixture card lists the players in the game. If a player scores a goal, we can place him at the game, but if he scores no goals, no link between player and game can be established. We need a new link.

In Figure 6-3, the link between *game* and *player* has been drawn on the ERM, as a many-to-many, because a player can play in many games, and a game involves many players. This many-to-many has to be decomposed. What linkage entity do we use? Does it need to be an artificial entity which serves

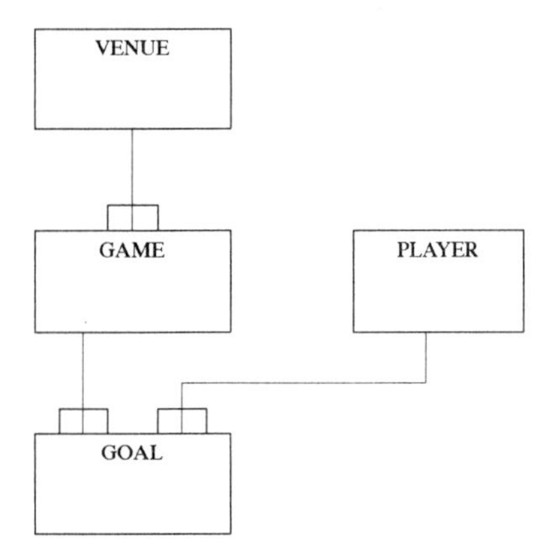

Figure 6-2 Five-A-Side: Improved ERM

Venues host games, goals are events which are associated with both games and the players who score the goals.

only to show the link between a player and a game? What would the link entity be called? How about *play-event* — or more simply, *played*? Would this link entity have any other attributes? The date the player played is in the *game* entity. All details of which player played are in the *player* entity. There seems to be no need for any other attributes in the link entity.

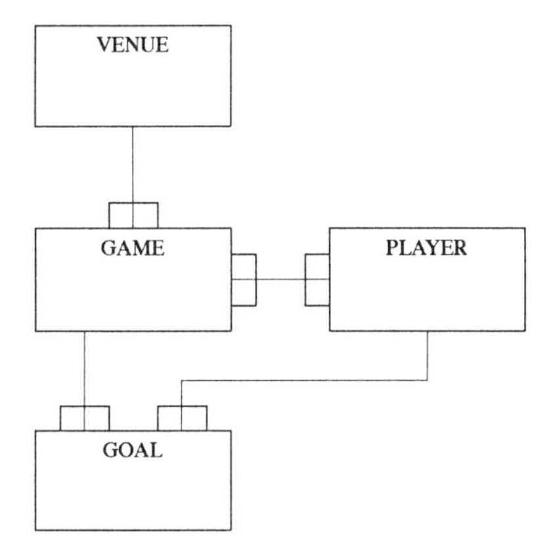

Figure 6-3 Five-A-Side: Play and Game Connected

Players must have a direct relationship with games. Not every player scores a goal.

This new entity serves another purpose. The entity *goal* should no longer to be linked to *game* and *player*, because it is the *played* entity, the player at a game, who scores the goal.

A registered player may be associated with the many times he or she has played, but the record of the player can only be associated with one and only one player. Since each player exists only once, we need to know about them only once.

A game relates to a number of players, usually ten, who *played in the game*, but the information about who played in the game will be associated with one and only one game.

A player is a person, and the entity *player* is of type: person. Games and goals are both events, taking place at a set time and date. *Game* and *goal* are entities of type: event. A venue is a physical location or place, with an address. *Venue* is an entity of the type: place.

We have now arrived at the final ERM for this case study (see 6-4). Some aspects of this ERM are further discussed in later chapters, but a study of the ERM diagram and the relationship rules in the next section will help to clarify many of the principles and issues of data modelling.

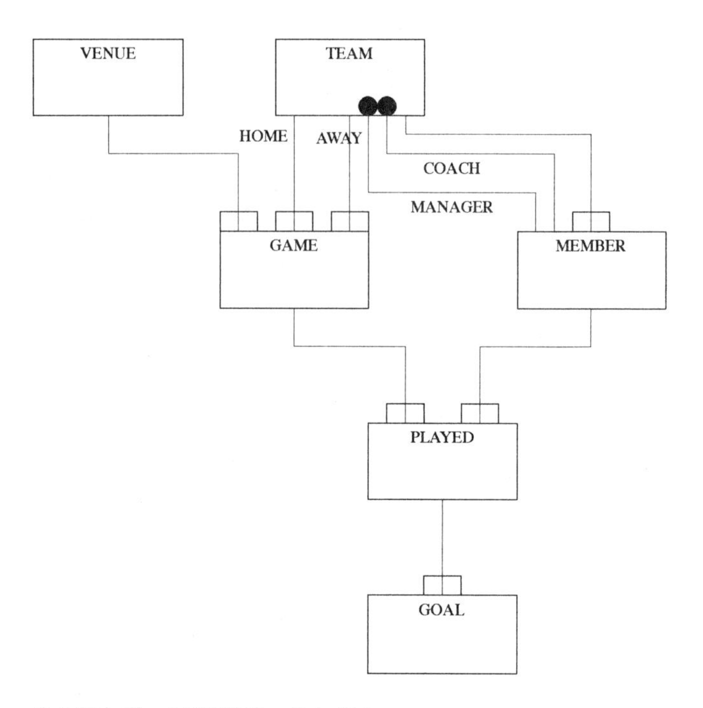

Figure 6-4 The Final ERM For 5-A-Side

Data Tables

It is about time to examine the tables by which we will implement this ERM. There are six tables, one for each entity, and each table has its unique identifier underlined. Also underlined in each table are the *foreign keys*, those keys which are the unique identifier of *another* table, and which form the links between tables. Foreign keys have the same name as the original unique identifier to which they refer, except where it is important to distinguish between foreign keys for clarity. These links are the implementation of the relationships in the ERM. There are nine relationships on the ERM and therefore nine foreign keys in the tables. It is important to realise that, in some cases, the foreign key forms part of the unique identifier of a table.

Team(Team-Name, Date-Formed, *Manager-Registration-Number*, *Coach-Registration-Number*)

Venue(Venue-Name, Address, Capacity)

Game(Game-Reference, Date-Of-Game, *Venue-Name*, Referee-Name, *Home-Team-Name*, *Away-Team-Name*)

Member(Registration-Number, Name, Address, Date-Of-Birth, Date-Registered, *Team-Name*)

Played(*Registration-Number*, *Game-Reference*)

Goal(*Registration-Number*, *Game-Reference*, Minute)

Foreign keys are in italics, in this set of tables only, to make them easier to spot. Data tables are often handwritten and italics are not normally used.

Relationship Rules

The list of relationship rules is an important aspect of the data analysis process. Experienced data analysts may well not record these formally, especially when they are dealing with a simple problem, such as those to be found in some of the case studies. However, even an experienced analyst will verify the design by checking the rules, if only mentally. For less experienced analysts, writing the relationship rules down is essential. There is normally a rule for each relationship shown on the ERM, and each rule has two parts, separated by a comma. The two parts each describe a *direction* in the relationship.

A team has zero,one or more members, but a member must belong to one and only one team.

A team has one and only one member as coach and one and only one member as manager, and a member may be coach or manager (or both) to one and only one team.

A venue may host zero, one or many games, but a game must be hosted by one and only one venue.

A *member playing at a game* may score many goals but a goal must be scored by one and only one *member playing at a game*.

> A member may be a *member playing at a game* zero, one or many times, but each *member playing at a game* must refer to one and only one member.
>
> A game may have a *member playing at a game* zero, one or many times (usually ten, in fact), but a *member playing at a game* must refer to one and only one game.
>
> A team may play in zero, one or many games, but a game must involve two and only two teams.

In the above rules, to allow comprehensible English, the entity *played* has been written as: *member playing at a game*. (See note 1 below.)

Notes

1. The event of a game and the presence of a member at the game who scores the goal gives us a rather abstract entity — *played*. In the relationship rules, it is awkward to refer to this link entity, as it has no noun. You will note that the phrase 'member playing at a game' is used in the relationship rules instead of a noun. This entity is the decomposition of the relationship between the entity *game* and the entity *member*. Without this decomposition entity (or link entity) the relationship between *member* and *game* is many-to-many. The relationship rule would be:

> A member may play in many games and a game may have many members playing in it.

The derived link entity *played* is the entity to which *goal* relates. Goals, although scored by the player, do not relate to the player directly. Clearly a player can only score a goal when playing. Since there is an entity — an event entity called *played* — it is to this entity that *goal* relates. (See the explanation of decomposition of many-to-many relationships on page 51.)

Following the rule that every relationship must have a relationship rule has forced us into the position of some rather tortuous language. It may be better to retain the original many-to-many rule. Certainly while discussing the ERM with the user, it is advisable to do so.

This also begs the question as to whether the phrase *member playing at a game* is not in fact the true name of the link entity. However, this would not look very good as a file name in a database!

2. There are a number of synonyms in the case study, which are traps for the unwary, or for those who have not been exposed to the real world of data modelling where there is a many-to-many relationship between the word for something and the thing itself. Note the following rule:

```
A thing may have zero, one or many names and a
name may relate to zero, one or many things.
```

Synonyms to watch for in this case study are:

- game, fixture, match
- player, member, footballer
- venue, ground, pitch, field

It is rare that any two terms are perfect synonyms. Language does not tend to keep two words where one will do. It is much more likely that there is a very subtle difference in the meaning between the two terms. Furthermore, these subtle differences may be different as understood by different users.

The only way to resolve the difficulties presented by apparent synonyms is to thoroughly understand each user's viewpoint and to define the terms adopted very clearly for the purposes of the system, thus imposing a degree of formality on the system which previously was not present. It is extremely difficult for the data analyst to avoid having some influence on the design of the system, albeit often in subtle ways. It seems inevitable that the observer changes that which is observed.

Having said this, the data analyst must make every effort not to impose preconceptions or misconceptions on the users' view of their system. While it is necessary and, to a degree, desirable, for the analyst to provide formality and structure to the system design, the analyst must avoid undue interference with it.

3. There is a multiple relationship, specifically a two-to-many, in the ERM, between *team* and *game*. This is because a game will always involve two and only two teams. This is a special case of many-to-many (N:M) where one of the *many* relationships is a fixed value. This special kind of link is discussed in more detail in the next chapter.

4. The entity *goal* contains the details of the scoring. In the interests of avoiding duplication, this information is stored nowhere else. It may seem

intuitively obvious that there should be stored an item called result or score with the game details. The reader will note, however, that this would be a duplication of information, since the score information can be derived by scanning the goal information. There is an issue here of performance.

There is an argument for storing the score information in the *game* table, perhaps as attributes away-score and home-score. If this were done, it would vastly improve the retrieval of the results for a game. It would however require special processing to summarise the goal information in the *game* table.

Furthermore, there would be a greatly increased likelihood of inconsistency of data. Because the same information is being stored in two different places, the possibility would exist that the two sources would not agree. If the two sources do not agree, which do you take as accurate? Whether or not the summarised information is kept depends on the behaviour of the system.

CITY FIVE A SIDE FOOTBALL LEAGUE	
CARDIFF BOBCATS	
MANAGER : J.HOBSON, 22, ACACIA AVENUE, WEST PARK, EASTHAMPTON (0222) 26262	TRAINER : PAUL HEARNEY, 55, WESTERN ROAD, EASTHAMPTON (0222) 67676
REGISTERED PLAYERS	
HARRY, P	
WATKINSON, M	STEPHENS, D
GALLAGHER, P	OLDHAM, J J
ALLDER, N	HARRISON, H
BALDWYN, H G	BOLTON, W
THOMAS, R	KEELER, J T

Figure 6-5 The Team Index Card

The Team Card contains the entities Team and Player. There is a one-to-many relationship between Team and Player.

FIXTURE CARD	
CARDIFF BOBCATS	VS NEWPORT BEARS
DATE : MONDAY 21ST JUNE 1992	VENUE : EAST PARK PITCH NO 2
SCORE 2:1	
PLAYERS	
ALLDER, N	CRABBE, M
BALDWYN, H G (22 MINS)	URQUHART, C
HARRISON, H	PATEL, R
OLDHAM, J J (33 MINS)	RUDGELY, H (18 MINS)
KEELER, J T	OWEN, F
REFEREE : MR JOHN CALLAWAY, 23 EASTERN AVENUE, WESTHAMPTON	

Figure 6-6 The Fixture Index Card

On the Fixture Card we find the entities Venue, Club, Goal and Played.

CHAPTER 7

ONE-TO-ONE

☐ **The One-To-One Relationship — Membership Effects on Key Positions — Entity Merging — Attribute or Entity? — Entity Splitting For Performance**

The One-To-One Relationship

A one-to-one relationship exists between two entities when each entity in the relationship can only ever be associated with one occurrence of the other entity. For example, an offer and a sale are distinct and separate event entities, and both would be stored in their own right. The relationship rule for the one-to-one relationship between *offer* and *sale* might appear like this.

```
An offer may result in one and only one sale,
and a sale must be as a result of one and only
one offer.
```

One-to-one relationships are not a common feature of ER models. There are situations, however, when such a relationship is perfectly valid and necessary. The example of offer and sale shown above is one such, which we will look at in more detail later in this chapter. The one-to-one situation has a number of interesting implications. A one-to-one situation can often be dealt with by the question:

- Can the two entities be merged into one?

Figure 7-1 A One-To-One Relationship

An offer can only ever be associated with one sale, and a sale must be associated with one and only one offer.

This requires that further questions be answered:

- Is membership compulsory for both entities in the one-to-one?
- Are all attributes and keys common to the two entities?

If the answers to these questions are 'yes', then almost certainly, the designer is not looking at two entities but one. The two entity boxes then become one box, and the designer chooses a new name which validly and meaningfully refers to both. There are cases, however, briefly explained below, where the designer may choose to keep the two halves of the entity separate, effectively treating the two logical entities as a single entity.

One-To-One Memberships

There are four possible combinations of membership of one-to-one. These are, for two entities A and B:

- both entities have mandatory membership
- both A and B are optional
- A is optional, B is mandatory
- A is mandatory, B is optional

Let's look at each of these in turn to see what to do with such situations. If some of the examples seem somewhat unlikely or forced, it may be that they are. One-to-one is not a common relationship in a logical data model and providing sensible, reasonable examples with which everyone will be familiar is not always easy.

Both Mandatory

Both A and B have compulsory membership of the relationship. For example:

> A roof must be associated with one and only one completed building and a completed building must be associated with one and only one roof.

The two entities are strong candidates for merging. They are probably one entity. Examine the two entities to see if they have an unique key in common, and whether the contents of one entity appear to be validly attributes of the other. If this is the case, the entities are candidates for merging. In the above example, any attributes of roof could be said to be attributes of building. Since every building always has a roof, what need do we have to store the attributes of roof separately? They could just as easily — and more simply — be kept in the entity *building*.

It may seem that a more sensible designer would never have supposed roof to be separate from building, but the example holds true in many situations. The example used is of everyday objects in order to make understanding easier, but in many data analysis and design situations things are by no means so clear and commonplace. It is very common for beginners in the art of data modelling to inadvertently identify two separate entities in the early stages of analysis and design. It is only when the design resolves to produce a one-to-one relationship that the true situation is revealed: the two supposed entities are in fact one.

When both entities have mandatory membership of the relationship, and they have been identified as distinct entities which must be kept separate, the relationship can be implemented by including the unique identifier of *either* entity in the other entity.

Both Optional

Both of the entities have optional membership of the relationship. For example:

> A plug may or may not be associated with one and only one socket and a socket may or may not be associated with one and only one plug.

> An artificial heart may or may not be associated with one and only one patient and a patient may

```
or may not be associated with one and only one
artificial heart.
```

In the above examples, no time tracking is present. We are considering only a snap-shot in time — now. No history of the relationships between plugs and sockets or hearts and patients is required.

In this case, the solution is to create a link entity between the two to describe instances of the relationship. This link entity will have only two attributes, these being the keys of both parent entities.

Alternatively, the designer, to economise on the number of files created in the database, may choose to embed the key of one entity in the other, the key concerned to remain blank until a relationship is established with the other entity. It clearly is equally effective to embed A's key in B or B's key in A. The choice of these two alternatives depends on considerations such as which of the two entities is linked to the rest of the data model, which entity is retrieved more frequently. The designer should be satisfied that the trade off is worthwhile between wasted (blank) space in the database and the saving of the overhead and space required to maintain the linkage file.

One Entity Mandatory, One Optional

This is the situation in which A is mandatory and B is optional or A is optional and B is mandatory. For example, it is possible to have a record of an offer, where no sale for that offer exists (yet), but every sale must have an offer from which it results.

In this case, since the offer will *always* pre-exist the sale, the link between the two tables must be established by reference to the offer. Physically, in the database, this relationship will be enforced by embedding the unique identifier of *offer* into *sale*. In the following table definitions, in which the table name is followed by a list of the attribute names, the unique identifier of *offer* has been inserted into the table *sale* as a foreign key.

Offer(<u>Offer-Number</u>, Client-Number, Offer-Details)

Sale(<u>Sale-Number</u>, <u>Offer-Number</u>, Sale-Amount, Purchase-Client-Number, Sale-Details)

Attribute or Entity?

The presence of an erroneous one-to-one relationship in an ERM is often due to the designer mistakenly identifying the attribute of an entity as another entity. There is a slightly philosophical question as to what an entity and an attribute are anyway. There are plenty of examples of this kind of confusion. There are often attributes which fit the definition of an entity and which have attributes of their own and a distinct existence, which can equally validly be seen as an attribute or set of attributes of another entity.

For example, a database of cars set up by the car manufacturer may well have colour as an attribute of car. A paint manufacturer might have colour as an attribute of paint. A graphics software company might include a list of 1028 preset colours from which the user can choose when creating presentation business graphics. The graphics software might include a facility by which the user can create a unique colour by fine tuning the percentages of the three primary colours. This new colour could then be named and saved to the list of colours by the user.

What would this colour be an attribute of? The answer to this question is that clearly, *colour* in this situation is an entity. It satisfies the criteria for being an entity, in that it is uniquely identifiable (by its name), it has attributes (its percentage of primary colours) and it is of interest to the user or user organisation. We have here an example of something that is an entity in one environment and an attribute in another.

This is very common. It is also very common for the data analyst to extract the details of an attribute, such as colour, from a table, such as *car*, and create a new table (often called a lookup table or classification table) containing the colour-code and the full description of the colour.

Car(Chassis-Number, Model, Engine-CC, Colour-Code,
Other-Details)

Colour(Colour-Code, Colour-Description)

The *car* table then contains only the Colour-Code. The *colour* table then holds the Colour-Code and Description only. The use of such a table to look up a code has a number of advantages:

- it saves space, by avoiding duplicating the text of the description — which may be quite long

- it allows validation of the colour-code on input, thus improving the integrity of the database
- it improves consistency on retrieval, by retrieving via a code, the description of which only needs to be recorded once

The question of whether this is a real or true entity or otherwise is a moot point and in practical data modelling an unproductive one.

As has already been said, there are no absolutes in the process of data modelling. The process of data modelling seeks to identify the model of an environment through its data flows, data stores and human or machine data manipulators. This model is then implemented as a part of the environment itself, and if it successfully fulfills its purpose, the data model is valid.

Keeping One-To-One Separate

A valid reason for keeping the two original entities separate is to reduce the size of the implemented file to manageable proportions by splitting it into two or more files on implementation. The designer must discuss with the user which groups of attributes need to be retrieved in order to perform the activities in their area of the business.

Another valid reason for keeping the two entities separate is because one of the files will hold frequently accessed attributes, while the other will hold attributes which are accessed rarely. Splitting the entity in this situation may improve performance.

For example, if the entities are kept separate, the mandatory-at-both-ends characteristic of this case means that we can include the key which links the entities in either entity. It is up to the designer. Probably the most sensible approach is to nominate a primary entity, the other 'half' becoming the secondary entity. The primary entity should be the one more frequently accessed. The primary entity is the entity by which access from higher entities will take place. The unique identifier required to link the two entities is already contained in both.

Snapshot or History

A one-to-one relationship is more likely to be valid in a snapshot situation. If the database has only to record the situation now or at one specific point in time, one-to-one relationships are more common.

When the element of history is introduced, that is, we require access to information about the relationships over a period of time, not only does the amount of data stored suddenly increase, but one-to-one relationships tend to turn into one-to-many relationships and one-to-many relationships tend to turn into many-to-many relationships, requiring decomposition or link entities to be created.

When considering one-to-one relationships, therefore, it is extremely important to clarify with the user whether information about history is required, and which particular relationships in the data model are to be time-tracked. Without this information, the data analyst cannot make a reasoned decision as to whether the one-to-one is valid.

One-To-One

Summary

- Valid one-to-one relationships are uncommon in data models. One-to-one relationships should therefore *always* be examined very carefully.
- Four membership patterns are possible between two entities A and B, affecting the position of the linking key item:

  Both A and B mandatory:

  Store key of one in either. Consider same unique key for both. Consider merging the entities into one entity

  Both A and B optional:

  Store keys in a link entity, unless performance is more important than blank spaces

  A optional, B mandatory:

  Store key of A (optional) in B (mandatory)

  A mandatory, B optional:

  Store key of B (optional) in A (mandatory)
- One-to-one relationships are often caused by mistaking an attribute of an entity for an entity in itself
- Distinguishing between an entity and an attribute can sometimes be problematical. Common sense and user needs should prevail
- One-to-one relationships may result from splitting an entity for performance reasons, possibly because some attributes are retrieved very frequently, some only very occasionally.

CHAPTER 8

ENTITY RELATIONSHIP MODELLING ADVANCED TOPICS

☐ **Positional Semantics — Hierarchical Diagramming — Four Combinations of Membership — Entity Merging — Multiple Relationship Lines — Recursive Relationships**

Positional Semantics

There would be very few dissenting voices to the statement that an ERM's fundamental purpose is to record and communicate meaning about a real world information system. The use of the ERM is sometimes referred to as *conceptual modelling*, because what we are doing when we derive an ERM of an information environment is modelling the *conceptual* structure. The use of the four syntax symbols of rectangle, line, degree symbol and membership markers are part of the semantic function of the ERM. Semantics means, broadly speaking, meaning. In this context, the rectangle, line, degree symbol and membership marker provide meaning.

In most ERMs, the position of the entities and the relationships is random. It seems a shame to allow randomness of this kind in a diagram the purpose of which is to record and communicate meaning. There has, however, been for some time a school of thought which suggests that all *many* symbols should be drawn pointing down the page. From the use of a crow's foot as a *many* symbol, this is referred to as using 'live crows', since the crow's feet are downwards and the crow is presumably standing up. Using the same metaphor, crow's feet drawn sideways are referred to as sick crows and the crow's feet which point straight up are dead crows. These are shown in Figure 8-1.

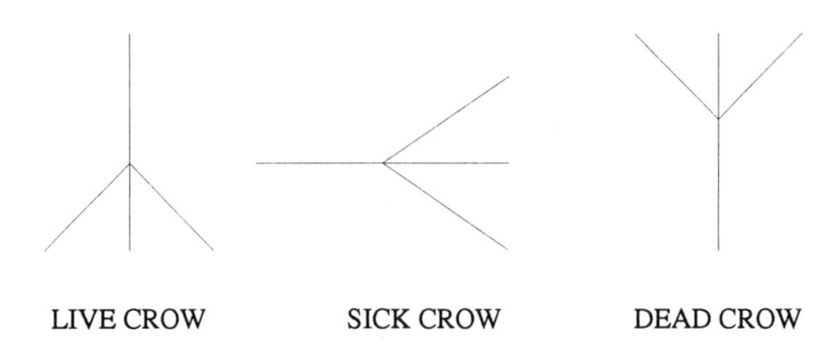

Figure 8-1 Crow's Feet

While these visual metaphors are somewhat quaint, there is a strong body which adheres to the use of the live crow metaphor. It is understood that some people who use ERMs are unconvinced by these metaphors, but there are a number of advantages to using exclusively top-down diagramming (live crows), as we shall see.

Hierarchical Diagramming

The approach of positional semantics means that the position of a diagram element in the diagram is significant and conveys meaning. From now on, the approach of positioning the *many* symbols so that they always point downwards on the page will be referred to as using the hierarchical diagramming approach. The very quaintness of the crow's foot metaphor may be responsible for some of the skepticism in the industry regarding its use, but many companies and practitioners in industry adhere to and teach this technique.

The benefits of positional semantics are as follows:

- Those entities which appear at the top or upper part of the diagram tend to be the master entities (those which are higher or highest in the ownership chain). Such entities tend to be the strong, hard, physical entities, and often the major entities about which the enterprise is concerned. Thus the position of these entities describes and confirms aspects of their nature.

- Those entities which appear at the bottom or lower part of the diagram tend to be the weak entities (those which are lower or lowest in the ownership chain). These entities also tend to be the softer, less physical entities, some of which exist only as link entities describing the relationships between two other entities, or which are decompositions of entities above them. (An example of this is the one-to-many between *invoice* and *invoice-line*). Thus the position of these entities also describes and confirms aspects of their nature.

- The ownership chains, the lines which run from the upper part of the diagram to the lower part, are easier to follow since they flow logically in one direction.

- The access paths, the lines which run from the lower entities to the higher entities, are easier to follow, and determining access via the membership markers is made visually easier.

- Comparison of two ERMs for the same real world information system is considerably easier, since they adhere to positional rules and will inevitably have a similar top-down layout.

- An M:M relationship in the ERM cannot be drawn if adhering to top-down diagramming. It is impossible to have an M:M relationship drawn with a straight line and both 'many' symbols pointing downwards. In this way, the top-down approach forces designers to decompose M:M into a form which can be supported in a relational database.

- Patterns in the ERM are more easily identifiable. For example, multiple crossovers, which may indicate a need to merge entities, are more easily visible using top-down diagramming. (Multiple crossovers are discussed later in this chapter).

Four Combinations of Membership

In his seminal book on data analysis and database design, Howe refers to the four types of possible membership combinations as A, B, C and D. These are shown in Figure 8-2.

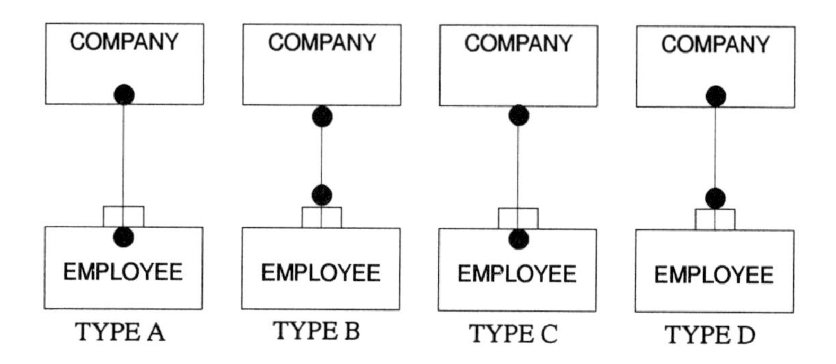

Figure 8-2 Four Types of Membership

The four types of membership, A, B, C and D are described by Howe (see further reading at the end of the book). Type C is far more common, and is the 'natural' relational membership. Type C is therefore termed 'default'.

The relationship rules for the four types are shown below.

A. A company must have at least one member of staff, and a member of staff must belong to a company.

B. A company may have zero, one or many staff, and a member of staff may belong to zero or one company.

C. A company may have zero, one or many staff, but a member of staff must belong to one and only one company.

```
D. A company must have at least one member of
staff, but a member of staff may or may not
belong to a company.
```

Default Membership

In real world information systems, the combination in Howe's type C is by far the most common of the four combinations of membership, and this is the one type of the four which is implemented in a relational environment without any need for extra link entities or extra rules in the database process. In this combination the parent or owning entity does not have to have a relationship with the lower entity, but the lower entity must be associated with the higher entity, as shown in the relationship rule for type C above. From now on, this combination will be referred to as default membership.

Designers should try to adhere to type C for simplicity. There is also a very strong argument for producing an ERM where only those relationships which do not adhere to the default membership are marked. Figures 8-3 and 8- 4 illustrate this point.

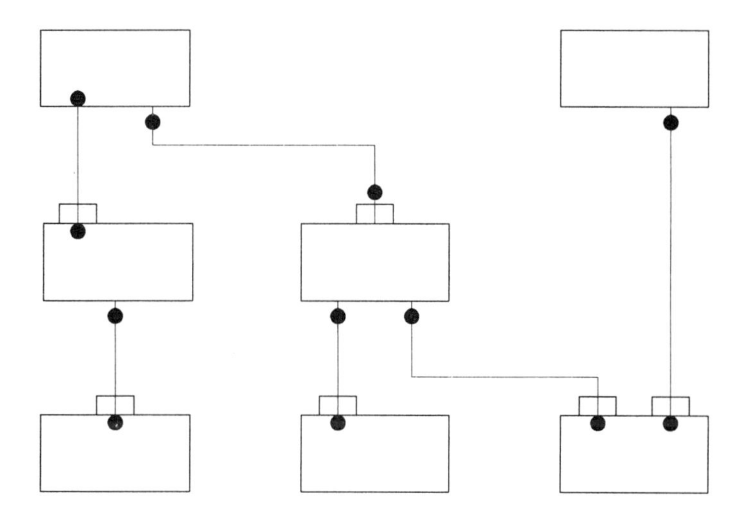

Figure 8-3 Fully Marked Membership

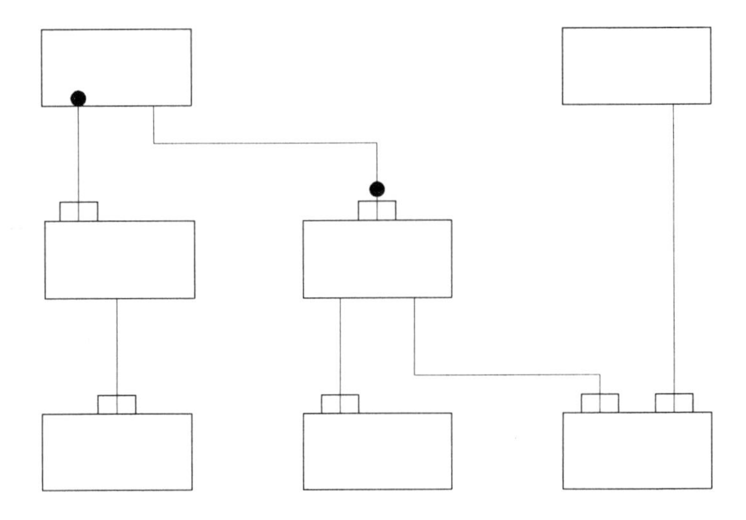

Figure 8-4 Non-Default Membership Marked

The advantage of only marking the exceptions are:

- The diagram is less cluttered than it would be if fully marked with all memberships.
- The exceptions (non-default memberships) to the natural relational model are clearly shown.
- The designer may tend to try and eliminate all exceptions to produce a more elegant diagram and an easier implementation.

If the designer attempts to eliminate as many exception markers as possible, this should not be done at the expense of the workability of the model. There is no suggestion that the ERM should be artificially manipulated to reduce the number of exception markers. There are cases, however, where the rules of the business are unclear or flexible and that, for simplicity's sake, it may be possible to eliminate exception markers without impairing the model's effectiveness. For example, the business rules may state that an order will always have at least one order-line, suggesting the membership of *order* in the relationship with *order-line* is compulsory. The designer has, however, the option of allowing the order (order-header) to exist even though an order-line has not been entered. This would adhere to the default membership and may be the preferred option. The final decision rests with the designer, after consulting with the user.

There is one drawback of using default-only marking of membership. It is conceivable that confusion could occur if a person reviewing the ERM thought that the absence of membership markers indicated that those memberships had not yet been considered or decided. This possible problem is easily resolved by noting in the diagram that 'Only non-default memberships are shown'.

Entity Merging

A common difficulty experienced by analysts occurs when two or more entities exist in the ERM, where one is sufficient to fulfil the needs of the model. It may be that the two entities in question have similar — or even identical — attributes, but because of the words used by users or analysts, the concepts — and the entities — remain separate. In the following example, the merging of two entities in an early version of the ERM is demonstrated, as well as a number of other interesting ways of moving from a first draft ERM to a more elegant and effective final version.

Let us first look at Figure 8-5. The paths between the upper and lower entities in Figure 8-5 are in the form of crossovers, where lines not only cross, but cannot be uncrossed by rearranging the layout of the diagram. A pattern in paths of this nature often (but not always) indicates that some merging of entities may be possible or desirable.

The relationships between the higher and lower entities have a large number of pathways and make the diagram very complex. It is frankly a mess. The model does, however, fit with the business rules of the environment of an estate agent. If this ERM were implemented as a database it would quite possibly support the business perfectly well. Check the business rules with the user to make sure. This is what the diagram in Figure 8-5 says in structured English relationship rules.

```
A vendor can be involved in many sales, but a
sale can only involve one vendor.
```

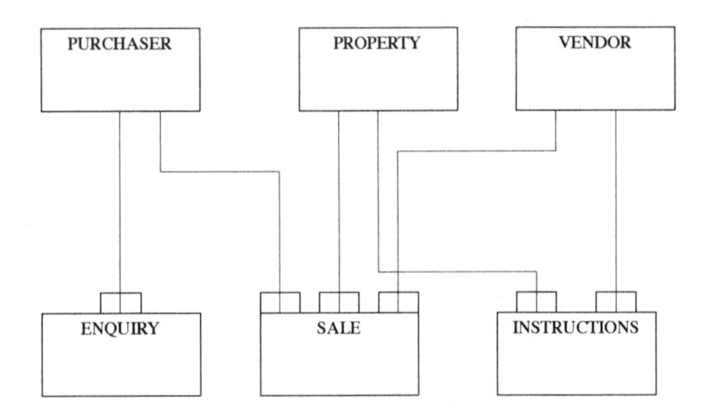

Figure 8-5 Estate Agent First Draft ERM

A vendor can give the business many instructions to sell, but an instruction to sell can only come from one vendor.

A purchaser can be involved in many sales but any given sale can only have one purchaser associated with it.

A property can have many instructions to sell associated with it, but an instruction to sell can only be for one property.

A property can have many sale associated with it, but a sale can only be of one property.

A purchaser can make many enquiries (that is, statements of a requirement and a desire to buy), but each enquiry can only be from one purchaser.

In these rules and for the purposes of this exercise, we are assuming that even though two or more people may jointly be buying or selling a house, that they are logically one vendor or purchaser. The business will only record the vendor or purchaser once, possibly with the names of all individuals stored together.

If we look at the ERM in Figure 8-5 more closely, we can see that the whole diagram would be greatly simplified if either some of the upper entities or some of the lower entities (or both) were merged. Let us look at this possibility.

(It is interesting to note that top-down diagramming (in which the many points down the diagram) serves to highlight this situation very clearly. If dead crows (many pointing up) and sick crows (many pointing sideways) were used, the appearance of the crossovers might not be so clear.)

It is clear that the entity *property* is quite different from *vendor* or *purchaser*. The attributes of a house are quite different from those of a person. There is no possibility of a merge here. However, the entities *vendor* and *purchaser* are not so different. They are both people. They may have identical attributes. It is time once again to ask the user about the business rules and the business information needs.

Is there any information kept about *vendor* or *purchaser* which makes them different from each other?

The only difference, our user tells us, is to do with the *enquiry*, the *instruction* to sell and the *property*. The nature of *vendor* and *purchaser* are not inherent in the entities themselves, but in the relationships with the lower entities in the diagram.

A *vendor* is not, then, distinguished from *purchaser* by any attribute, but by the fact that a *vendor* has a relationship with an *instruction*, where a *purchaser* has a relationship with *enquiry*. *Instruction* and *enquiry* are different entities anyway. Let us then merge *vendor* and *purchaser* into a new entity *client*. (See Figure 8-6.)

In Figure 8-6 we can see that the diagram has already been improved. We have eliminated an entity. We now have two relationships between *client* and *sale*, those of vendor and purchaser. As shown in the ERM these two relationships must be explicitly labelled, to distinguish between them. There are always these two relationships between a sale and the business' clients. The use of multiple paths between two entities is discussed a little later in this chapter.

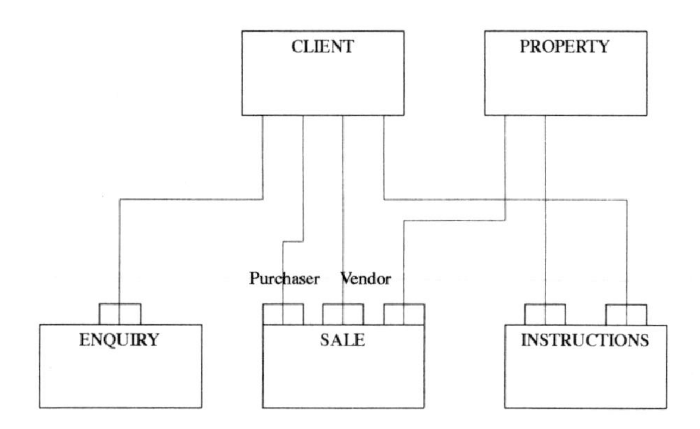

Figure 8-6 Estate Agent Vendor and Purchaser Merged

Purchaser and Vendor have been merged into one entity called Client. No other real changes have been made. Although some connections have been redrawn to improve the appearance, all relationships remain as before.

The ERM still looks messy but it has one less entity. This is nearly always a good sign. Generally speaking the more elegant and simple an ERM looks, the more likely it is to be easily implemented. In database design as in other branches of engineering, a simpler and more elegant solution, more pleasing to the eye, is often a better solution.

To confirm the ERM we must now go back again to the user. What are the relationship rules implicit in this new version of the diagram, and does the user still agree with them? Here are the relationship rules for Figure 8-6.

> A client can be involved in zero, one or many sales, as vendor or as purchaser (but not both in the same sale), but a sale must involve two and only two clients: one as purchaser and one as vendor.
>
> A client can give the business many instructions to sell, but an instruction to sell can only come from one client.

```
A property can have many instructions to sell
associated with it, but an instruction to sell
can only be for one property.

A property can have many sales associated with
it, but a sale can only be of one property.

A client may make zero, one or many enquiries
(that is, statements of a requirement and a
desire to buy), but each enquiry can only be
from one client.
```

The relationships in the diagram still cross over but we still haven't looked at the possibilities for merging lower entities in the diagram. Let us look now at *sale*, *enquiry* and *instruction*.

It seems unlikely that any of these entities can be merged. Intuitively, they are all quite different things in the estate agent's information environment. However, experience might suggest that two of these entities, while not identical, are intimately associated.

Consider the following relationship rules.

```
For each instruction from a client to sell,
only one sale can ever result.

For each sale of a property, there can only
ever be one instruction to sell which is
associated with it.
```

Check with the user. Are these true? If so, the relationship between *sale* and *instruction* is one-to-one. The reason why the one-to-one cannot be merged is that one sale results from an instruction, and has different attributes. However, the fact that we have identified the one-to-one does mean that we can simplify the data structures still further.

In Figure 8-7, we have only slightly rearranged the paths (still adhering to the top-down modelling approach).

Although we have reduced the number of relationships in the diagram, we have not lost any information. The relationships described in Figure 8-5 are still there in Figure 8-7, some explicit, one of them implicit.

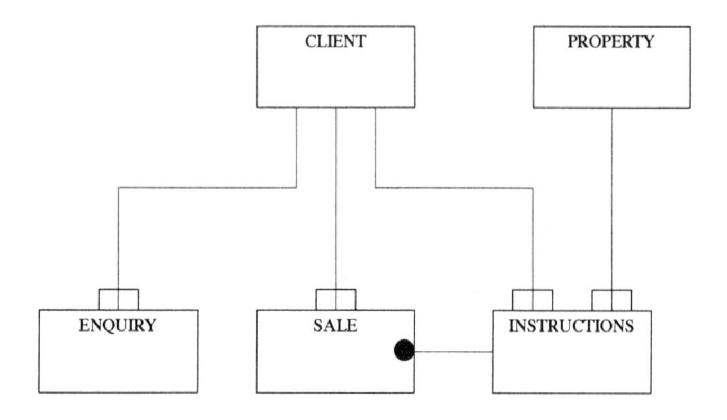

Figure 8-7 Estate Agent Final ERM

The relationship line between Client and Sale represents the Purchaser and the relationship lines between Client and Instruction and between Instruction and Sale represent the Vendor.

We have eliminated the double relationship between *client* and *sale*, thereby returning to the standard of unlabelled relationships throughout the ERM. The *client* entity's vendor relationship with *sale* is now implicit through *instruction*. After all, the person who instructed the estate agent to sell is going to be the one who is the vendor when the sale happens, surely? (Even if the instruction to sell is received from a solicitor, the vendor is still the client.) We must check the solution again with the user. Are the relationship rules still true and will the ERM still support the business functionality? A slight repositioning of the lower entities on the ERM gives an ERM with no crossovers at all.

The diagram now shows the mandatory nature of the link between *instruction* and *sale*. This is necessary because ERM convention states that all 'one' ends of relationships are by default optional. In this case, a client does not have to be associated with an instruction, an enquiry or a sale, but instructions, enquiries and sales must be associated with clients. In the one-to-one relationship between *instruction* and *sale*, common sense tells us that an instruction can (indeed must) exist without a sale, but for a sale to have occurred, an instruction to sell must previously have been received.

This is what the diagram in Figure 8-7 says now.

> A client can give the business zero, one or many instructions to sell, but an instruction to sell can come from one and only one client.
>
> A client may be involved in zero, one or many sales but any given sale must have one and only one client associated with it.
>
> > (The *client* vendor is implied by the one-to-many relationship between *client* and *instruction* and the one-to-one between *instruction* and *sale*.)
>
> A property can have zero, one or many instructions to sell associated with it, but an instruction to sell can be for one and only one property.
>
> For each instruction from a client to sell, only one sale can (optionally) ever result and for each sale of a property, there must be one and only one instruction to sell which is associated with it.
>
> A client can make many enquiries (that is, statements of a requirement and a desire to buy), but each enquiry can only be from one client.

If the relationship rules and the functionality support are indeed confirmed, we have moved from the early version (Figure 8-5), a messy, complex diagram with 6 entities and 6 relationships, to a much more elegant solution in the final version (Figure 8-7) with 5 entities, 5 relationships, no crossovers and one non-default membership. Not only is the situation simplified, but the solution is more rigorous and will impose the business' rules on its data structures more cleanly. The diagram explains the nature of the business data structures more clearly and even has an element of the business functionality (*sale* is one-to-one with and after *instruction*) implied within it.

This is a very good example of what can be done by checking for merge possibilities in an ERM. It is essential to check anything which looks like a crossover in the diagram, as well as examining one-to-one relationships carefully. It would be going too far, perhaps, to say that if two relationships have to cross in a ERM diagram that there may be something wrong. However, it always seems to be beneficial to try to flex or rearrange the diagram to dispose of crossed lines.

At the risk of appearing overly repetitive, it must be stressed that the solution described is not universal or even general. The solution is workable because it adheres to the business rules as expressed in the relationship rules. This particular example was derived after several interviews with senior staff at a major estate agents and after detailed examination of a representative set of real business documents. The model fits the working practices of *this business at this time*. The rules will change with the gradual evolution of the business. No ERM is right or wrong, just workable or unworkable and more or less elegant and efficient.

Multiple Relationship Lines

It has been explained that the standard solution to a many-to-many relationship is to decompose the relationship into a link entity to record the M:M occurrences. There is, however, an alternative method of dealing with the M:M problem, which is valid in a small number of special cases. This method involves drawing multiple relationship lines between two entities.

The use of more than one path between the same two entities can only occur when the two entities have an N:M relationship, where N and M are two different numbers and one of the numbers has a fixed, known value. Although any two numbers are candidates for N and M, the two-to-many relationship is the most common. An example of this can be seen in use in Figure 8-6 in which the relationship between client and sale is 2:M. The relationship rules for this arrangement are as follows.

```
A client may be involved in zero, one or many
sales, either as vendor or purchaser, and a
sale must involve two and only two clients. A
client must not be both vendor and purchaser
to the same sale.
```

This relationship rule is one exception to the ERM rule that each relationship line on the ERM diagram must have its own relationship rule and that an relationship rule must represent one relationship line. A second statement has been made, specifying that the same client cannot be both purchaser and vendor at the same time for the same property. This seems sensible, but only the individual estate agent would be able to confirm this rule. Furthermore, the designer should think twice before trying to implement the second part of the rule. Unless the rule is enforced in the database, there is a possibility of loss of data integrity, but the overhead of maintaining extra non-default rules, which may have to be written in the form of triggers, or worse still, as code in an application program, would have to be taken into consideration.

The two keys can sometimes provide a unique identifier for the entity. If there is a rule that there is only one *leg* of a sea voyage defined as being between, say, London and Antwerp, then the use of these two ports makes the *leg* unique. In the case of a *squash-game*, the rule must be that two players can only play each other once (for example in a league), in order for the two *player* keys to provide a unique identifier. In such a case, the order of the two keys is significant, and the first key must contain the highest player key (whether alphabetic or numeric) and the second key contain the lower player-key in order to ensure uniqueness.

In producing an ERM we are looking for a meaningful model which allows maximum understanding. We do not want a proliferation of pathways in our diagram. Although, for example, the number of players (on the field) in a rugby match is always 30, it would not be very elegant to have 30 relationship lines between the entity *rugby-player* and the entity *rugby-match*. In this case, the M:M would almost certainly be decomposed by a link entity such as *player-match*.

When two or more relationship lines are drawn between two entities, the lines must be clearly labelled. This is not an exception to the general rule that labelling of relationships is only necessary when the possibility of confusion or ambiguity exists. Ambiguity would certainly exist if the multiple relationship paths were not labelled. (See Figure 8-8.)

The use of the multiple path is an obvious option in some specialised cases of entity relationships. The relationship rules for a squash game are given as an example:

```
A player may play in many games, but a game
must involve two and only two players.
```

The multiple path implies that there will be two attributes of the *many* entity which will contain keys of the *two* entity. The option to use multiple relationship lines is available to designers but should be treated with caution.

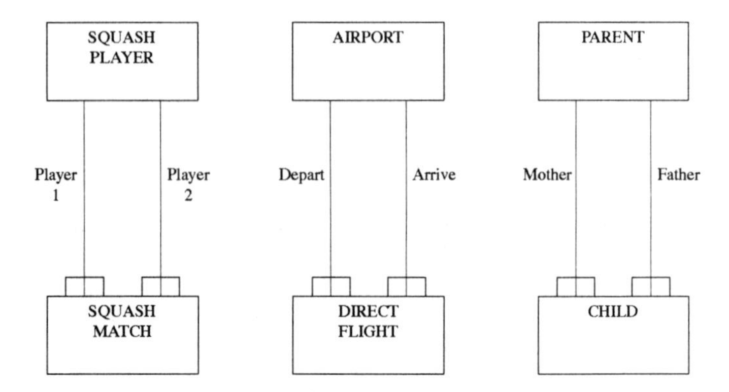

Figure 8-8 Examples of Two-To-Many Relationships

Two or three relationship lines between two entities is reasonable, but more than this may detract from the understanding of the ERM.

It is important to realise that the implementation of an N:M relationship can be perfectly adequately achieved by using a link entity as for the general case of M:M relationships. The database would provide the same information whichever solution was used. The designer must consider the performance of the database and the benefits of simplicity of design in making the decision as to which solution to use.

Recursive Relationships

There are a number of special cases or circumstances where an entity has a relationship, not with another entity, but with itself. This kind of relationship is called recursive. Consider the following examples:

> A sub-division of a company (such as a division, department or section) may contain many other sub-divisions of the organisation, but each sub-division of the organisation belongs to one and only one other sub-division of the organisation.

> An identifiable assembly of parts in a machine may contain one or many other identifiable

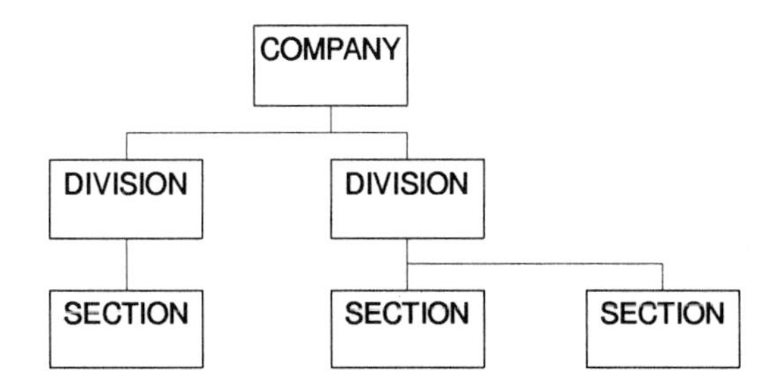

Figure 8-9 An Organisation Structure Of A Company

A company is an example of an hierarchical structure. Another example is the Bill of Materials containing parts and assemblies. Hierarchical structures are also known as Tree structures

```
assemblies, and an assembly may be a part of
many other assemblies.
```

In investigating the company in Figure 8-9, the designer discovers that the attributes of *company*, *division* and *section* are all the same. Clearly, these are occurrences of a single entity. In such cases, where the entity is heirarchical — the recursive relationship is the best way of modelling the business environment (See Figure 8-10). Data analysts often refer to such relationships as 'bill-of-material relationships', because the bill of materials — the list of parts which make up a part at a higher level — is the most common and

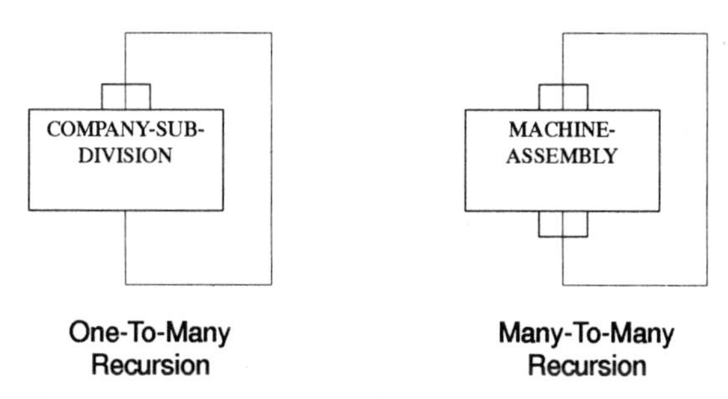

Figure 8-10 Examples of Recursive Relationships

A Company-Sub-Division can contain many Company-Sub-Divisions below it inthe hierarchy, but only belongs to one Company-Sub-Division, above it in the hierarchy

A Machine-Assembly may contain many Machine-Assemblies and may be contained in many Machine-Assemblies.

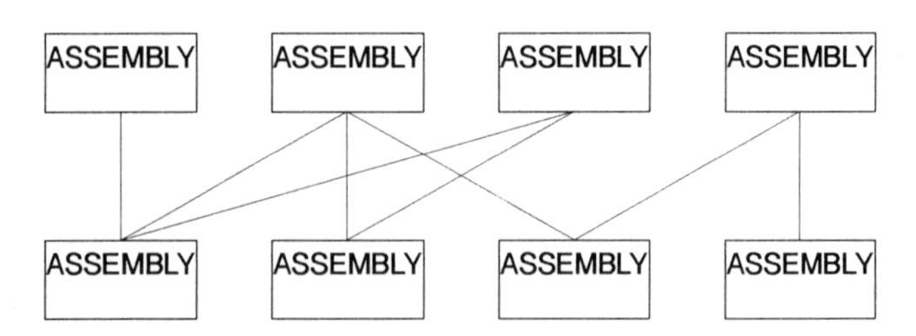

Figure 8-11 A Bill-Of-Materials Structure

A Bill-Of-Materials is an example of a network structure. Bill-Of-Materials structures are commonly found in engineering manufacturing.

obvious example of many-to-many recursive relationships.

The two two kinds of recursive relationships — one-to-many and many-to-many — are examples respectively of an *hierarchical* structure and a *network* structure. An hierarchical structure is like a tree, with a single root and many branches. A network is, generally, a structure in which any member can connect to any other member, although some networks may restrict in various ways the associations of its members.

Implementing Recursive Relationships

In the case of a one-to-many recursive relationship, the relationship is implemented by inserting the key of the table into itself, to show the occurrence's relationship with the occurrrence immediately above it in the hierarchy of the organisation.

> Company-Sub-Division(<u>Company-Sub-Division-Name</u>,Company-Sub-Division-Description, <u>Member-Of-Company-Sub-Division-Name</u>)

In a one-to-many recursive relationship table, there will always be one and only one occurrence where the Member-Of item is blank — the highest level of the hierarchy or the *root*.

When the designer has recognised a many-to-many recursive relationship and has modelled it correctly, it is implemented by use of the following kinds of data table:

Machine-Assembly(Assembly-Code, Assembly-Description, Other-Assembly-Details)

Part-Of-Assembly(Assembly-Code, Contained-In-Assembly-Code)

where the Assembly-Code is an unique identifier, but the Contained-In-Assembly-Code is the unique identifier of another *assembly*. The first table is the implementation of the entity *machine-assembly* itself, the second table is the link entity which resolves the many-to-many.

Recursion is a subtle idea in data modelling, but a very important one. Where an occurrence of an entity may contain or relate to another occurrence of the same entity, it is the only sensible way of dealing with the problem. The business or organisation may then make an enquiry of the database by retrieving on either the first, unique key, or the second *contained-in* key. In this way, whether the structure is a hierarchy or a network, we can produce — for any member or occurrence — a list of the members or occurrences contained within it.

ERM Advanced Topics

Summary

- Positional semantics, the method of diagramming all 'many' ends of relationship lines downwards, is widely used in industry. It provides additional meaning in the diagram, and assists both navigation within the diagram and comparison of solutions in the same environment
- Crossed lines in the ERM may often be eliminated by

  changing the layout of the diagram
  merging entities
  designing a more elegant solution
- ERM diagrams may be simplified and improved by merging entities. Entities with the same attributes may be candidates for merging
- Multiple relationship lines between entities may be necessary and desirable
- Recursive relationships exist when an occurrence of an entity relates to another occurrence of the *same* entity. Such constructs are neccessary for modelling heirarchical relationships.

CHAPTER 9

LOGICAL DATA DICTIONARY

☐ **Data Tables — Database Creation — SQL Data Definition and Data Query Language — Metadata — Normalisation — Logical and Physical Data Dictionary**

Data Tables

In the process of data modelling, we are moving towards a final result: the data tables — often in the form of a data dictionary. It must be stressed that this chapter is complementary to the chapters on entity relationship modelling, entity life histories and data flow diagrams. These are not separate subjects, but aspects of one subject — data modelling. None of these topics can be properly understood in isolation from the others.

A data dictionary is the definition of a set of interrelated data structures which are used to create the database itself. The data dictionary is composed of the definitions of a number of tables, themselves composed of a number of columns of data. The data dictionary determines the nature of the data items themselves — their type and size, and may include information about the limitations on the data which can be accepted and stored in these columns. The data dictionary may also define which items are to be indexes and the linkages between tables using these indexes.

Database Creation

Once the process of data modelling has produced a workable design, in the form of a logical data dictionary, the data dictionary, or a subset of it, is used to create the database itself. Some databases require the data dictionary to be entered by filling in screen forms with the WIMP (Windows, Icon, Mouse, Pointer) or cursor and text method. Other databases simply take the typed text of the data dictionary statements and use them to build the database files and indexes which will hold the data.

SQL

SQL (or Structured Query Language) is a database manipulation language which, although a little primitive as database languages go, is widely accepted as a standard, making it quite popular. Although a detailed coverage of SQL is beyond the scope of this book, the data definition and data retrieval capabilities of SQL will be used to illustrate the implementation of data tables and how data is retrieved using SQL.

The logical data dictionary, once completed, is translated into *create* statements which tell SQL which files are to be built and their structure. The create statement given below defines the name of the table, the names of the items in the table and the type and size of the items.

```
create table drivers
        (surname            char(20) not null,
        driver_no           char(10),
        date_of_birth       number(4));
```

Surname is defined as being of type character (char) and of length 20. Driver_no is 10 characters and date_of_birth is a four digit number. Other types of data are available in SQL, and the reader may obtain more information about data types in the books in the reading list at the end of this book.

Whichever database management system is being used — and there are quite a few — these statements will be executed and the files built. The database management system will also store, in its own internal dictionary or repository, information about the format of the data taken from the *create* statements. Later in this chapter, an example of an SQL enquiry is given, to demonstrate the retrieval of data from the database and to show how the relationships in the ERM and the resulting key linkages in the tables are used to join tables together for retrieval. In the case study chapters later in this book, the SQL *create* statements for the ERMs and tables are given.

Table Names

For the sake of consistency and in order to adhere to standards, it is a very good idea to settle on one specified way of naming tables. Firstly, the table should have a name which clearly describes the nature of the data in the table — in much the same way as we named entities earlier. Entities were named as a single noun. In order to distinguish between entities and the tables which store the information about the entity, we shall be using a plural noun for naming the table. A data table which contains information about cars, for example, could be named *cars*. Likewise, a table containing information about customers would be called *customers*.

Indexes

An index is, as is normally understood by the word, a way of obtaining immediate access to a particular record in a set of records. When we say that a set of index cards, for example, is stored in alphabetical order, we are saying that any index card can be quickly found by searching on a particular alphabetical item on the card, rather than having to separately examine each card in turn.

Computers use a separate file for the index, which maintains the ordered sequence of the records. New records added to the main file of data are stored in the order in which they were put into the file — serially.

In a computer system a file can be sorted into a particular order, as a card file might be. This method requires the entire file of records to be reorganised every time a record is added or deleted and is generally unsuited to a computer database, because of the enormous amount of processing required. For the purposes of data modelling, you can think of an index as a way of making a set of data records appear as if they are sorted in a particular order, to facilitate retrieval of a particular record.

Metadata

Metadata is data about data. It is the collection of information about the information to be stored in the database.

There are a large number of issues which should be addressed by the logical data dictionary. The definition of the data should be as detailed and as clear as possible. The names of the tables, the names of the data items which make up the columns of the tables, the type and size of the data items are normally mandatory in order to build the database itself, and the syntax of the data definition language will normally require these.

Some data definition languages allow far more metadata to be stored in the data dictionary, and if this is the case, obviously the data designer will want to take advantage of these more detailed definitions. If the data definition language allows these extra items of information to be held, it is likely that other tools in the database facility, such as the screen generator and the checking of the input from input statements will use this definition, making the job of the programmers much easier.

The storage of metadata can greatly improve consistency of quality in a database. For example, if a particular item were defined as being composed only of the numeric characters 1-9 and 0, and this definition was stored in the logical data dictionary, then any screen in the application software which allowed this item to be entered by the user could automatically detect and enforce this definition. If, subsequently, the data analyst in conjunction with the user decided that any combination of numeric or alphabetic characters was allowed in the data item, the logical data dictionary could be amended accordingly and all screens would recognise and enforce the change automatically. This kind of capability, however, is only present in some database management systems.

Even if the database management system is not able to store or automatically enforce metadata definitions, they should not be neglected. Programmers will, instead, write the programs which enforce the metadata, and will need a well-maintained logical data dictionary from which to obtain the definitions.

Some of the kinds of metadata which should be considered by the data designer and which may be recognised and acted upon by the database application programmers or even the database management system itself are as follows:

- INITIAL VALUE
  This specifies the value which the item will have before the first input by the user. In order for this value to be different from the initial value, the user has to enter something different. This would be used in cases where a value is nearly always a particular value.
- DEFAULT
  This specifies the value the data item adopts when the user does not enter a value when prompted. If the vast majority of

customers, for example, have class 'R', then the default for the data item customer_class could be defined as R. This would allow the input operators to simply press a key in this field on a data input screen to accept the usual value for the field. This feature would reduce typographical errors and save time and effort.

- RANGE
  This specifies that the number in this data item must lie between two specific values in order to be acceptable. A data item such as price, for example, could not be negative and would not be zero. The business may well want to define that a price cannot be greater than a certain value, in order to avoid typographical errors. This is a definition which could be of great benefit to programmers when building validation routines for certain data items. Some database management systems may automatically validate the item on input, rejecting it if the input value lies outside the given parameters.
- BLANK WHEN ZERO
  This specifies that a number of value zero is to be output as a blank instead of a zero character.
- OUTPUT FORMAT
  This defines the format to be used for output of the item to screen or printer. For some data items, such as telephone numbers, there is often a standard format for output. The area code may be a four digit number in brackets, with the remaining numbers grouped in twos or threes.

The data item telephone number, stored as, for example, 0987445422 might be defined as TELEPHONE-NUMBER CHARACTER*10 OUTPUT FORMAT "(####) ### ###" and would appear as (0987) 455 422 on the screen or in a report.

This format could be defined in the data dictionary, allowing either the automated facilities in a fourth generation environment or the human programmers to use the definition and maintain consistency. It is obviously not a good idea to store the spaces and brackets in the database itself. This would take up a lot of unnecessary space.

- SCREEN LABEL
  This specifies the label, an alternative name for the data item which will be used when the screen generator creates a screen format. Screen generators are fairly common facilities in fourth generation database systems, but many screen generators default to the item name in the dictionary and only allow the label to be changed on the particular screen layout. This would mean that labels could become inconsistent from screen to screen and that any change to the label of an item would have to be explicitly changed on every separate screen referencing the data item. It is clearly preferable, if the label is to be different from the data item, that the label is defined once only. Even if the database management system does not have screen generators which recognise dictionary entries which distinguish between the data item's name and its label, it is good practice to specify this in the logical data dictionary so that programmers can maintain consistency.
- COLUMN HEADING
  This acts in the same way as screen label above, but applies to reports produced for the printer.

These metadata definitions are not always necessary for each data item, of course. On the contrary, some of them will be only very rarely required. The benefits which accrue from the data designer considering these detailed issues about the data to be stored in the database are quite significant, and a good data designer will include those extra definitions that are necessary for consistent and accurate data in the data dictionary.

Third Normal Form Tables

No discussion of data modelling could possibly be complete without an examination of normalisation. Having reached this point in the book, the reader has seen a number of fairly basic points about the tables which are derived from the data modelling process:

- Each data item in a table must be dependent only on the key of the table. This means that for a car, for example, if you have the registration number, you can access the record for that particular unique car and find out what its colour or engine-capacity is.

- Each key value of a table must reference only one item of data in each column of the table. It would be unhelpful, to say the least, if we accessed a table by a unique registration number and obtained 157 different engine capacity values *for the same car*.

Normalisation is a set of rules which arose from set theory, the theoretical and mathematical basis of data modelling. These theories put forward a number of rules of which only the first three are normally used. A third normal form table is a table which obeys the first three rules of normalisation, which are discussed later in this chapter.

Normalisation is a technique of data analysis which requires the analyst to determine the dependencies between all the items in the data sets. It is a very cumbersome and non-intuitive method, which is normally only used in situations where the data items and entities are very complex and difficult to understand or when the methodology demands it. In most data modelling exercises it is sufficient to use the rules of normalisation to verify the design produced by the entity-relationship modelling process. This verification is achieved by answering the following three questions:

- does each data item in the table depend *entirely* on the key of the table?
- does each item in the data table depend on the *whole* key of the table?
- does each data item in the table depend on nothing *else* but the key of the table?

This is perhaps better understood by using the often quoted corruption of the legal oath:

> each data item should depend on the key, the whole key and nothing but the key of the table, so help me Codd. (Ted Codd is one of the 'founding fathers' of database design theory.)

First Normal Form Rule

First normal form rule is that all the data items in a table must depend on the unique identifier or key of the table. The unique identifier of a table must control or determine every item in the table. Every time a row is found by means of the unique identifier of the table, we must find the same value for every item in the table. Therefore, there must be only one data item in a table cell (the intersection of a row and a column).

The rule that the unique identifier of the table must directly control every data item, involves the removal of repeating groups from the table. This means that if a data item occurs more than once for one occurrence of the unique key or identifier of the table, it must be removed into another table.

For example, if the rules of a business state that, over a period of time, more than one driver may drive a car, and we wish to track this one-to-many relationship over time, it would be incorrect to keep any items of data about a driver in the table *car*. Given the business rule that many drivers can drive a car, in the table *car* below, Driver-Number is a repeating item.

Car(Registration-Number, Colour, Make,
Date-Of-Registration, Driver-Number)

Driver-Number, and all other items to do with the driver, belong in their own table — *driver*.

Second Normal Form Rule

The second normal form rule is that all items in the table must depend on the whole of the unique identifier or key, not just part of it. Part-key dependencies are therefore removed. In a table where the unique identifier or key is concatenated — that is, made up of several items, all items in the table must depend on the whole key.

Order-Line(Order-Number, Line-Number, Product-Code,
Quantity-Ordered, Order-Date)

In the above table, Order-Date depends on Order-Number alone, not on the whole key of the table *order-line*. To leave Order-Date in this table would break the rule for second normal form. A table where the key is a single item, of course, is already in second normal form.

Third Normal Form Rule

The third normal form rule is that no items in a table may depend on anything other than the key. Items which depend on another item which is not the key (inter-data dependency), are therefore removed.

Order(Order-Number, Customer-Number, Customer-Name, Order-Date, Salesman-Code, Salesman-Name, Delivery-Code)

In the above table, there are two cases of inter-data dependency. Customer-Name depends on Customer-Number alone, not on the key of the table *order*. Likewise, Salesman-Name depends on the item Salesman-Code, not on the key of the table *order*. The items Customer-Name and Salesman-Name belong in their own tables.

This example, incidentally, clearly shows one of the fundamental differences between the top-down data modelling approach of entity relationship modelling and the bottom-up approach of normalisation.

In the entity modelling approach, both *customer* and *salesman* would have been identified as entities at an early stage, and the above table would never have come about.

Unnormalised Data

Unnormalised data is data which has not been tested against the first three rules of normalisation and which does not obey these rules. For example:

Car (Registration-Number, Colour, Driver-Name, Engine-Capacity)

This simple table, containing only the names of the data items, would be said to be unnormalised, if the item Driver-Name does not depend on the Registration-Number of the car, *in the real-world information system which we wish to model*. In some cases, it may appear to do so. In a simple database belonging to a business which issues company cars to some employees, the driver's name may indeed be validly stored as an attribute of car, as a column in the table *car*.

In this business database it is the car which matters, and the driver is stored only in association with a car. In this database, entering a registration will retrieve the car's details, including the person currently assigned to drive the car. In the database for the Driver and Vehicle Licensing Centre in the UK, however, the registered keeper is the person associated with the car, not the driver. The driver is normally determined by the driving licence number.

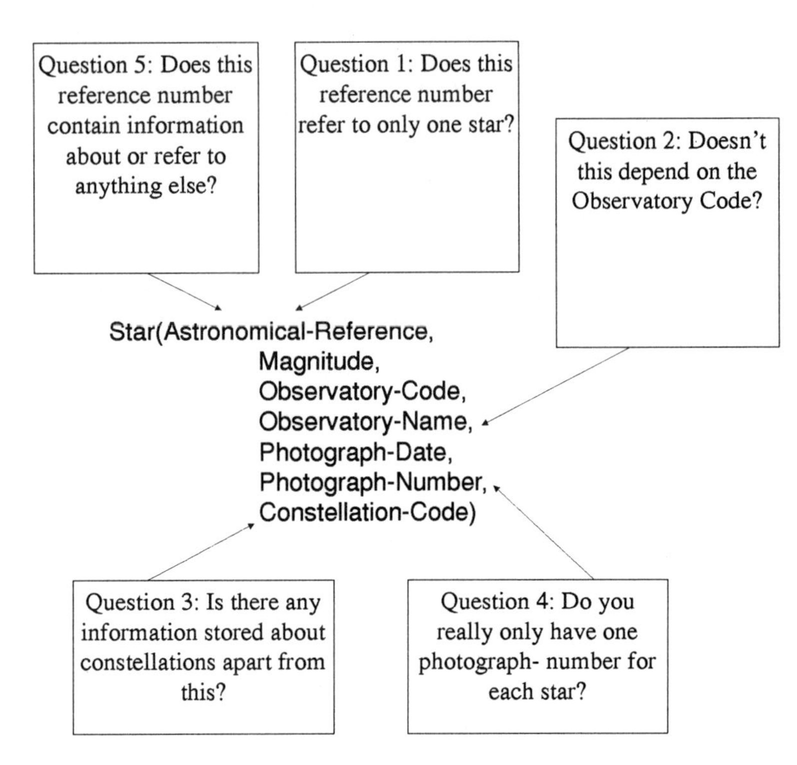

Figure 9-1 Verifying that Tables are Well-normalised

It is impossible to give a clear rule about what data items depend on other data items in a database, without a clear understanding of what the database is for and how the information is to be viewed.

In Figure 9-1, there is a simple data table about a star. Perhaps this table has been extracted from an astronomer's card index file, or from some sort of document. The figure illustrates some of the questions which the designer must ask in order to be sure that the table is in third normal form. The data designer must never, never, assume knowledge about a data environment.

Physical Data Dictionary

The physical data dictionary is the implementation of the design in the data dictionary in the computer itself. This book is about data modelling and cannot address all of the physical data dictionaries — produced by a wide range of hardware and software companies — into which the design could be implemented. Nearly all systems will have SQL at the very least, but may well have their own means of defining the data. They may use a menu-driven, form-filling interface, or a DDL or Data Definition Language. All such database or dictionary systems will have clear instructions in their manuals as to how to translate a solid design into the physical dictionary.

Denormalisation

Denormalisation is the process — carried out after the logical data design is complete — of deciding where to break the rules of normalisation for the sake of performance. In many business and organisational environments, the data held — even in relational databases — is often partly unnormalised. Unnormalised data is data that has never been properly normalised in the first place. Denormalisation may be carried out to improve performance by reducing the number of files and linkages that have to be stored or by reducing the linkages needed between certain tables during a common report program run.

For example, the user may wish to have very frequent analysis, on line, of customer invoices. Rather than slow the process down — perhaps to an unacceptable level of system response time (SRT) — the data item Customer-Name may be included in the *invoice* table, along with the unique identifier Customer-Number.

It may seem strange to go to all the trouble of designing a logical ERM, only to reverse the process, to effectively degrade the design, but this is exactly what happens in actual database design implementation.

It could be said that the data modelling process ends with a good, working ERM and set of tables. It is also true that a well-informed data analyst will know better where to denormalise, and where not to, than someone not trained in data modelling.

Relational Database Enquiries

Relational Databases operate by storing their data in a number of tables and by maintaining a number of links between these tables. Each table holds the data about an entity of the system and the links or keys between the tables hold the relationships between the entities. When the users need to access the information held in the relational database, the access is achieved by means of an enquiry. This enquiry must be asked in a language which the database management system recognises and must be framed in terms of relational functions carried out on the tables.

Because SQL is the most widely recognised data query language and has an established standard across all computer systems, the example is given in SQL.

```
select surname, registration, start_date
from driver, driven
where driver.driver_no = driven.driver_no
and end_date = 0;
```

The above SQL *select* statement demonstrates how the foreign key — representing the relationship between two entities — is used to join the two tables together. In Figure 9-2, the shaded portion of the two tables represents that part of the two tables which will be retrieved by the above SQL statement.

The statement has a number of clauses. The first clause contains the *select* verb and the list of data items to be retrieved. These data items may be extracted from any of the data sets or stores accessed, and will be displayed

Driver		
Driver-No	Surname	DOB
JON1235	Jones	12.1.55
SMI5434	Smith	1.5.62

Driven			
Registration	Driver-No	Start-Date	End-Date
A123XYZ	JON1235	17.7.88	21.3.90
A123XYZ	SMI5434	22.3.90	
POW456T	SMI5434	13.6.91	
POW456T	JON1235	7.12.90	
GHI 98 X	BRO5432	8.11.91	9.7.92
G 111SSD	BRO5432	7.6.90	9.6.90

Figure 9-2 The SQL Enquiry In Action

The table Driver and the table Driven have been joined via the key data item Driver-No. Only certain columns and certain rows have been selected, as specified in the SQL enquiry statement.

in the order in which they are requested without regard to the order in which they are physically stored in the datasets.

The second clause begins with the keyword *from* and lists the data sets or stores which are to be accessed.

The third clause in the SQL statement shown is the *where* clause. The phrase

```
where driver.driver_no = driven.driver_no
```

specifies to the database management system that the two datasets are to be linked by the data item given, thus forming a joined set of records. The dataset name is given first, followed by a point or full stop followed by the name of the data item. In plain English, this phrase might be written: where the driver-number in the table *driver* is the same as the driver-number in the table *driven*. This clause is central to the concept of relationships between entities and is the actual implementation in the database of the relationship.

The phrase

```
and end_date = 0
```

instructs the database management system to retrieve only those joined records in which the end-date is zero — those cases where the driver is still driving the car.

In Figure 9-2 where the two tables *driver* and *driven* are shown, the arrows indicate the effect of the join and the shaded cells of the tables show those data items which will be retrieved. The result of the enquiry will be as follows:

Surname	Registration	Start-Date
Jones	POW456T	7.12.90
Smith	A123XYZ	22.3.90
Smith	POW456T	13.6.91

This example of SQL retrieval code is given only for the purpose of demonstrating how relationships between entities in data modelling are actually used in a database management system. The syntax and use of SQL for the creation, manipulation and retrieval of data from a database management system is beyond the scope of this book. SQL is a subject in its own right and the reader will find details of books which deal with SQL in the reading list at the end of this book.

LOGICAL DATA DICTIONARY

Summary

- The logical data dictionary is the repository of metadata: data about the data to be held in the completed database.
- The logical data dictionary is a set of textual statements which are the table definitions, comprising a name for the table, a list of data items to be held in the table, with information about each item to be held.
- The item definition in a data dictionary will be composed of the item name, its type, its size, and may hold other information about the data item such as its allowable range, the way it is to be stored physically, the way it is to be displayed to the user, its initial or default value or a pattern or definition against which it is to be tested before being accepted from the user.
- Normalisation is the bottom-up approach of considering the dependency of all data items and deriving tables which obey the rules of normalisation.
- First normal form rule

  each cell (intersection of row and column) in a table must contain only one data item
- Second normal form rule

  all items in the table must depend on the whole of the unique identifier or key, not just part of it
- Third normal form rule

  no items in a table may depend on anything other than the key
- Denormalisation is the process of deliberately breaking the rules of normalisation in a database, to improve performance or for some other implementation reason. Unnormalised data is data which has never been normalised and which may break the rules of normalisation.

- SQL is a data definition language (DDL), used to define, in the database management system, the name of a table and the name, type and size of the items in the table.
- SQL is also used to retrieve data from tables in a database management system by specifying which columns and rows are to be retrieved and joining tables via the keys. The joining of tables via keys is the physical implementation of relationships between entities.

CHAPTER 10

DATA FLOW DIAGRAMS

- **What Is A Data Flow Diagram? — Purpose Of DFDs — Data vs Functionality — Understanding The Information Environment — Diagram Elements — General Rules — 'Legal' and 'Illegal' Flows — Zero Level DFD — Decomposition Of DFDs — Conservation of Data**

What is a Data Flow Diagram?

Data Flow Diagrams (DFDs for short) are diagrams which show the flow of data from one place to another. DFDs describe the processes of a system, showing how these processes link together through data stores and how the processes relate to the users — the outside world. They are used to record the systems analysis as a part of the design documentation. At their lowest level of detail, as we shall see, DFDs are often included in a programmers working specification when the systems analysis is complete and the system is being programmed.

Also, and perhaps most importantly, DFDs are used by the analyst to communicate the understanding of the system to the user, to get confirmation of the design.

For example, here is an illustrative dialogue between a data analyst and Mr Smith, who is an order processing clerk.

In Figure 10-1, is the DFD being shown to Mr. Smith.

'Mr Smith, you have explained what is involved in accepting an order from a customer. This diagram shows that process, which we have called ACCEPT ORDER.

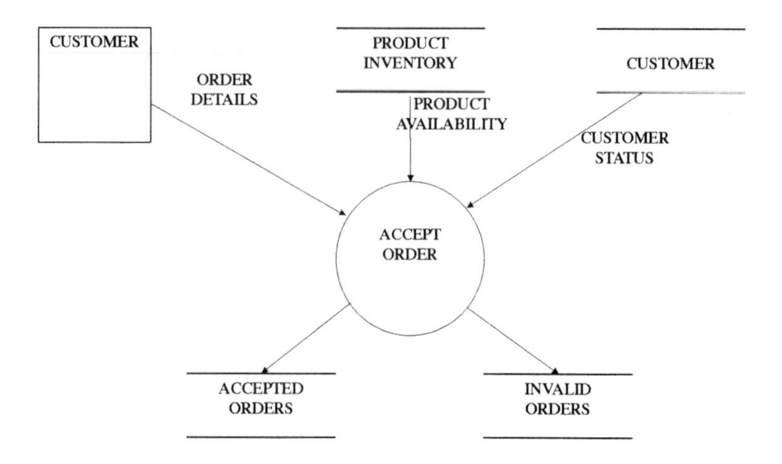

Figure 10-1 Data Flow Diagram for ACCEPT ORDER

The diagram shows that the order is received from the CUSTOMER, outside the system, and that the process needs to check a number of things. Firstly, the diagram shows that CUSTOMER STATUS is needed from the CUSTOMER file. Secondly, it shows that PRODUCT AVAILABILITY is need from the PRODUCT INVENTORY FILE. Here, the diagram shows that there are two places to which the process can send the order information: to the file ACCEPTED ORDERS or to the file INVALID ORDERS.

Mr. Smith, is that right?'

'Yes', says Mr Smith. 'That seems to be right.'

Don't worry for the moment about the diagram and how it is drawn. We will look at this in detail later in this chapter. The point of this example is to show

how a DFD is used by the analyst to show the user what the analyst has understood from the user's explanation of the process or function in question.

One of the great advantages of the Data Flow Diagram as a modelling technique is its simplicity. Unlike flowcharts or structured English algorithms, DFDs are readily understood by users with little or no understanding of computers or systems analysis. Thus, the DFD can be used for communication with the user — and communication with the user is the first and most important link in the chain which results in a valid data model and a successful system. If this link fails, the whole chain fails.

Data vs Functionality

The production of DFDs, while a part of the systems analysis approach as a whole, is also an integral part of the data modelling process itself. The data to be held in the system can never be seen as separate from the processes which use it. There are some views which suggest that a strong core representation of the data structures of an environment should be without reference to the processes to be achieved in the environment. That is, that an analysis which focuses on data is a far better approach than an analysis which focuses on the processes (the functionality) of a system.

This is true, but if an analysis of the processes or functionality is carried out in conjunction with (usually one step behind) data analysis, it will highlight inconsistencies (which may or may not be errors) between the data and functional analyses. A conflict between a DFD and the ERM might arise by revealing, for example, that a necessary process requires a data store which does not appear in the ERM resulting from the data analysis. When this occurs, the data model may be changed, or the process may be changed. The conflict must be resolved. For this reason, full data analysis and design should not be considered complete until the higher level DFDs, at least, are complete. The various levels of DFD are explained later in this chapter.

Understanding the Environment

The analyst, however well trained and experienced, cannot possibly know as much about the user's information environment as the user does. The only way for the analyst to understand what is going on is to ask the user, and to study the user's everyday working documents. These include both documents relating to the safe-keeping of information — card indexes, files, lists, archived documents — and documents showing how the information is processed by the user. The analyst will also identify where information comes from and where it goes to.

After carrying out this analysis, the data analyst will produce a set of DFDs which describe the flows of information in the situation under study. These DFDs can then be shown to the user and the user can confirm, or otherwise, that they are correct. (However, be warned that different users may disagree on the correctness of the same DFD, and even the same user may realise later in the analysis that some aspect of the DFD has been misunderstood or was forgotten.)

Process Analysis for DFDs

The elements of the DFD as a diagrammatic tool are very simple, and so are most of the rules governing the construction of DFDs. What is not simple is how to understand the system or that part of the system you are trying to analyse, so that you can record that understanding in a DFD. There is absolutely no short cut to understanding the system. This takes time, effort, skill and experience.

The data analyst has to examine all relevant documents, hunt down all the documents that have been missed or that the user forgot to mention, thoroughly study and analyse all the existing data stores and talk to the users (all of them) who are involved in the part of the system being studied.

Furthermore, the analyst will almost certainly have to reconcile the different explanations from different users. This will mean either resolving these different views by identifying different names or terms for the same thing or actually discovering conflict in the real world information environment and persuading management to help change those working practices or views of the system which are creating the conflict.

It is not and could not be in the scope of this book to teach data analysts how to understand how a system operates. This an entirely different topic, which requires a study of management strategy, business practices and business management, law and economics, accounting, salesmanship and an endless range of business related studies. Even after undertaking such studies the data analyst will never be a good data analyst until he or she has developed a strong foundation of experience of information systems in all their variety. In this chapter we will only be looking at the DFD as a technique or method of recording and validating the analyst's understanding of the information system.

DFD Elements

Data Flow Diagrams are essentially a very simple kind of diagram. Unlike flow charts, DFDs have very few elements in them. DFDs contain only the following elements:

- data stores
- externals
- processes
- data flows
- system boundary
- (optionally) physical flows

The diagram is made up of these elements only, drawn and linked together to show an integrated whole. The shapes of the elements — the way that they are drawn — differ from place to place and from methodology to methodology. The principles, however, vary little and the data analyst, having mastered one convention for producing DFDs, will have little problem in adapting to a new methodology or new working practices in a new working environment.

Those readers with some previous experience in systems analysis may note that there is an element they have seen before which explicitly does not appear in the previous list of DFD elements — the decision box. That is because decisions are *not* recorded in DFDs. A DFD is *not* a flow chart. At no time do either-or logical decisions play a part in the construction of DFDs.

DFDs simply show what flows of data move to and from processes in a system. No implication whatever of sequence of events or flows of time is included in a DFD.

Decision-structured diagrams, such as flow charts, imply a flow of time as well as a flow of information. In a flow chart, a process is carried out, *then* another process, *then* another. In a DFD, this is not the case. Those analysts who are used to working with flow charts may find this conceptual transition from flow charts to DFDs difficult, but it must be achieved.

Data Stores

Data stores in a DFD represent the places where information is stored. In an information system these may be filing cabinets, a sheaf of paper in someone's drawer, a computer file or any other form of storage, including human memory. The data store is named with a single noun. The name should represent, clearly and unambiguously, the nature of the information held. This element of the DFD is very similar to the entity seen in previous chapters.

Data stores are represented in a DFD by a two parallel lines with the data store label between them (see Figure 10-2).

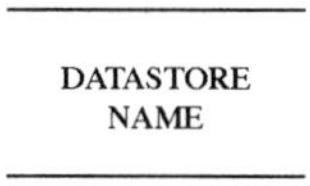

DATASTORE
NAME

Figure 10-2 The Data Store Symbol (Parallel Lines)

Externals

These elements of the DFD represent external sources of information and external targets to which information goes. Externals are outside the system which is being studied. Examples of externals are *customer* and *supplier*. It is very important to distinguish between the externals and the data stores. It is perfectly possible — even likely — that there will be externals with the same name as a data store. This is because the people or organisations who send information to the system and who receive information from the system are almost certainly represented in a data store inside the system, in order to keep up-to-date information about the person or organisation. A system which has an external called *customer* will also have a data store called *customer*.

Externals are represented in a DFD by a square with a label inside it. (See Figure 10-3.)

EXTERNAL
NAME

Figure 10-3 The External Symbol (Square)

Processes

Processes in a DFD represent a point at which data is changed in some way or sent from one place to another. Processes show manipulation of the data. A process may be shown at a very high level, such as a process called 'PREPARE INVOICES' or may be split down into much smaller processes which make up the higher level process. Analysing a process and splitting it up in this way is called 'decomposition'.

Processes are represented in a DFD by a circle with a label inside it. (See Figure 10-4.)

Figure 10-4 The Process Symbol (Circle)

Data Flows

Data flows in a DFD represent the movement of data from one place to another in the information environment. In the DFD, they connect the other three types of element (externals, processes and data stores) together. Data flows do not, under any circumstances, modify, change or otherwise make any difference to the data that is flowing. Because DFDs are so simple, there are only a few ways the data flow can connect other elements:

- external to process
- processes to data stores

and conversely

- processes to externals
- data stores to processes

DATA FLOW NAME

Figure 10-5 The Data Flow Symbol (Arrow)

Data flows are represented in a DFD as a labelled arrow from one element to another element. (See Figures 10-5 and 10-6.)

In some cases, it is neither necessary nor desirable to label the data flows. These are exceptional cases, and the general rule is to have labels on data flows. In those cases where, in the opinion of the data analysts and to the users, it is completely obvious what data is flowing from one element to another, the label can, and should, be omitted.

The data flow in Figure 10-6 is carrying the customer data to be stored from the process which is storing it to the customer data store. Is it really necessary to label the data flow 'customer data'?

Data stores, externals and processes must always be clearly, simply and unambiguously labelled, but, as in this example, it may not always be necessary to label a data flow.

Many practitioners of data modelling take the view that data stores are directly analogous to entities in the ERM and to files in the resultant Logical Data Dictionary (LDD) and that often in a DFD, all the data associated with an entity flows in or out of the data store whenever it is accessed. Many practitioners also take the view that the storage data flows, since they all start or end at a data store are often really 'access' indicators, indicating not exactly what data is flowing, but that the data flowing is coming from or going to a certain data store. The programmer can read whatever data from the store or write whatever data to the store as is necessary to complete the process task, but all the data — the entire entity — is accessed, and all attribute values are available. If the DFD is at a low enough level (part of the programmers' working specification) to require such detail, the name of the process reading or writing the data usually makes it clear exactly what subset of the total entity data is involved.

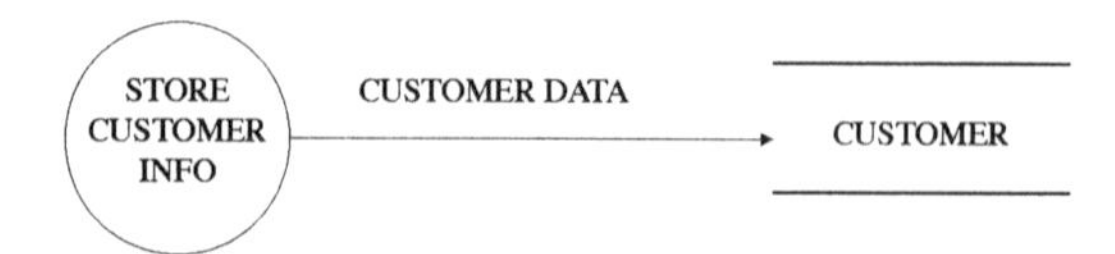

Figure 10-6 The Data Flow In Action

This Data Flow Diagram shows a flow of customer data from the process called 'Store Customer Info' to the data store called 'Customer'.

The general rule, as always, is break the general rules with care, and always for the purpose of greater clarity. A diagram clutteredwith text is not necessarily more clear than a diagram which has less wording, but, if in doubt, label the data flows.

System Boundary

The system boundary, although not an element as such, is often included in a DFD as a line (sometimes dotted or dashed) which surrounds those elements which are within the system, and which excludes externals. This is really a duplication of information, because externals are always outside the system, and there is no real need to show, diagrammatically, the boundary. However, redundancy can be useful to ensure clarity and confirm understanding, and a system boundary line can be used if desired.

The inclusion of a system boundary is also useful to distinguish flows to and from the system (to and and from externals) from those flows *inside* the system. Since these particular data flows are the interfaces with the outside world, they will be of particular importance for the image or goodwill of the company or organisation and should be subjected to highest levels of quality control.

The system boundary is shown in a DFD as a line surrounding the system and excluding the externals. An example of a system boundary can be seen in Figure 10-8.

Physical Flows

Physical flows are mentioned here because a number of DFD methodologies and approaches include them. They are used to represent the physical flow of some object or material thing between elements. For example, if your company were to send out a purchase order to a supplier, the data analyst might show the subsequent movement of the goods ordered as a physical flow from the external called *Supplier* to an external called *Goods Received.*

Since DFDs are *Data* Flow Diagrams, it is highly questionable as to whether physical flows should play a part in a DFD. The general rule, as always, is that the more informative the DFD is the better.

Physical flows are represented in a DFD as a labelled double arrow linking an element to another element. Only externals can be linked with physical flows. (See Figure 10-7.)

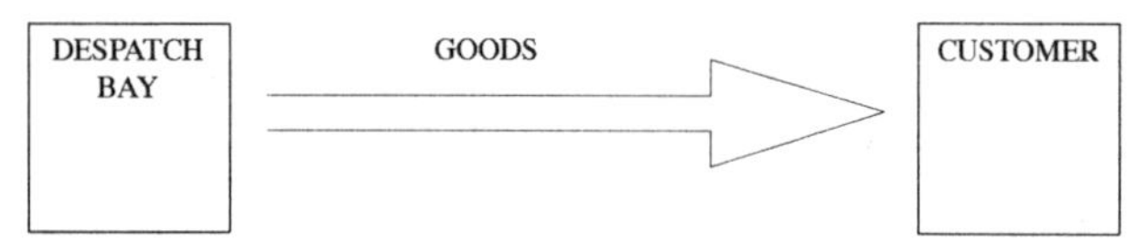

Figure 10-7 The Physical Flow

Illegal Data Flow Linkages

Some possible permutations have not been mentioned above. They have not been given as elements which can be linked together by data flows because they cannot be so linked. The reasons why are simple. These permutations are:

- External to data store
  cannot be linked because externals (such as *customer*) cannot insert their information into a data store (such as *customer* or *order* without any action (process) in the system. Even if the customer were permitted to update orders using a computer link, it is a fact that no data store in a computer can be

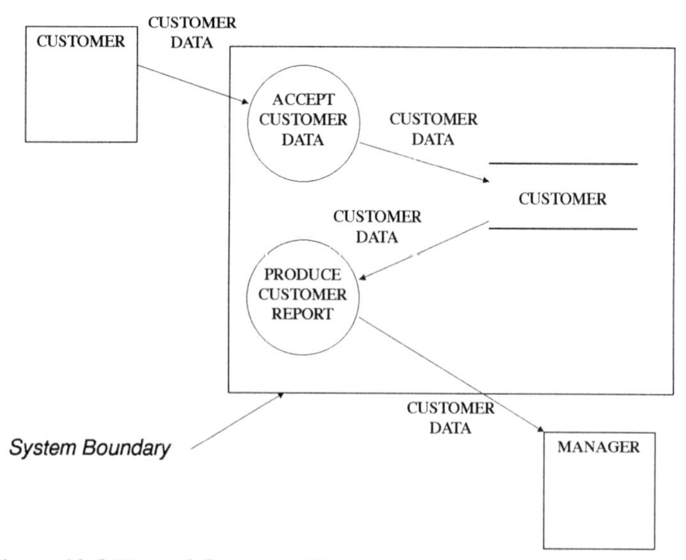

Figure 10-8 Flow of Customer Data

changed without a process being involved.

- Data store to external
  cannot be linked because a data store cannot output information without a process being involved to read the store. Certainly, no designer would want to imply that data can leave the system without any control from the system!

- Process to process
  Although processes can and do pass data to other processes, it is arguable that this is advisable in any system. It may be better to store information in an intermediate data store (either temporary or permanent), for clarity, for audit purposes and for integrity or security. It could be said that processes which directly exchange data are not truly separate processes and should not be shown separately on a DFD.

  When constructing DFDs for the purpose of data modelling, we are focusing closely on the data requirements and data structures to be used for storage. In this case, it may be unnecessary to distinguish between two processes if no storage of data occurs between them. Certainly, when DFDs are used to define the modular structure for programs, as they are in detailed process design, data flows between different processes are quite commonly used by data analysts.

- Data store to data store
  A process is *always* necessary to read from or write to a data store. Otherwise, how does the data get from one data store to the other? Furthermore, if the data is flowing from one data store to another without being changed (remember that data flows never change data), the data is being duplicated, which breaks a fundamental rule of data modelling.

- External to external
  Data flowing from one external to another external is doing so outside the system and should not be documented as a part of the system.

These 'illegal' data flows are generally undesirable, and should not be used without much thought. However, the function of the DFD is to represent a visual, diagrammatic view of what is really going on in the real world information system. Rules are necessary for guidance, but if the data analyst properly understands the reasons for the rule, the rule may then be broken in the interests of clarity and understanding.

Zero Level DFD

Data Flow Diagrams have levels of detail. Each process circle as drawn represents some form of action or manipulation of information within the system under analysis. At the highest level, there is only one process — the system itself in its entirety.

A zero level DFD is the simplest possible DFD. It has a number of unique characteristics, which distinguish it from lower level DFDs:

- It has only one process, the system itself.
- It shows no data stores, as all these are contained in the process - in the system.

A zero level DFD shows only the one process, the system, and its surrounding Externals, with the named flows to and from the system. (See Figure 10-9.)

The zero level DFD is often called a *scope* or *context diagram* because it shows the scope or the context of the system. The zero level DFD is a simple form of requirements specification because it describes every input to and output from the system, effectively describing at a very high level exactly what the system will (and by implication will not) do. The scope or context diagram, when used to define at an early stage the inputs and outputs from the system, nearly always precedes the data analysis and data modelling phases of systems development.

Decomposition of DFDs

Within the zero level DFD, the scope diagram, there are many other processes which together make up the system. One process can be broken down into its smaller constituent processes. In this, the principle of modularisation is clear. When designing anything, it is wise to start by examining the whole thing, then to break the complexity down into simpler and simpler units. In this way, the units arrived at are more manageable and more easily understood by both designer and user.

In the construction of Data Flow Diagrams, the same principle applies. The zero level DFD — the system as a whole — is divided up into meaningful sub-processes, and these in turn may divided yet again.

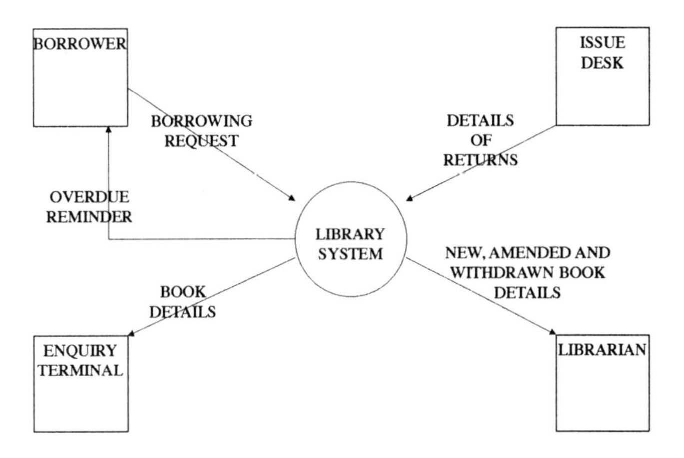

Figure 10-9 A Scope Diagram

Conservation of Data

The conservation of data is a general, and unbreakable, rule when constructing DFDs. It states:

It is impossible in any system for data to be created, destroyed or altered without the involvement of a process.

The data analyst must always be aware of this rule and must check the DFDs as they are constructed to ensure that, at no time, does a DFD imply that a data flow changes data, or that data appears from nowhere, whether a process is involved or not.

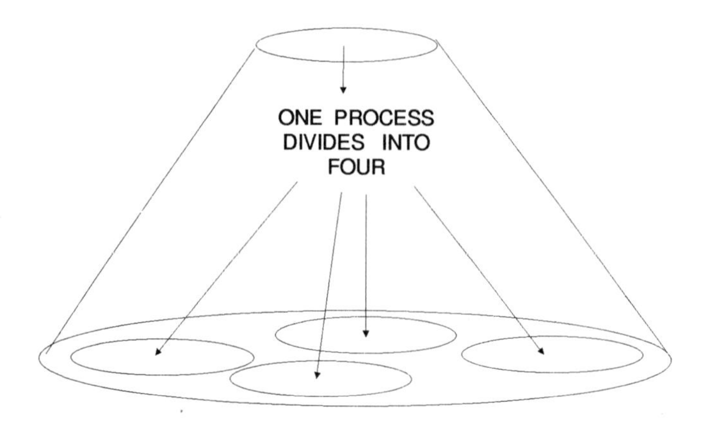

Figure 10-10 The Decomposition of a DFD

DATA FLOW DIAGRAMS

Summary

- Data Flow Diagrams are a graphical representation of the flow of information inside an information system design
- Data Flow Diagrams are composed of only the following elements

  data stores (labelled parallel lines) analogous to entities

  externals (labelled square)

  processes (labelled circle)

  data flows (arrows) which should be labelled if the data which is flowing is not implicit

  system boundary

  physical flows

- The zero level DFD (also referred to as a scope or context diagram)

  has no data stores visible

  has only one process — the system itself

  can be used as a simple, early specification device

CHAPTER 11

ENTITY LIFE HISTORY

☐ **The Entity Life History — Processes and Events — Nodes — Sequence, Selection and Iteration — Level of Design Detail**

The Entity Life History

The Entity Life History (or ELH) is a diagram showing all the things that can happen to an entity during its lifetime. Just like any other thing, an entity has a birth event, when it comes into existence, a death event, when it ceases to exist and other events which affect it, change and examine it. Charting these events can be a very important aspect of data analysis. The ELH tells us, by implication, all the other entities which interact with the entity being examined (some of which may have been missed altogether during the early stages of analysis) and all the aspects or attributes of that entity which are accessed or affected. It may also imply some of the rules which control addition, update or deletion of the entity.

All entities undergo change within the system. These changes will be in the form of processes in the system that impact on the entity, changing its state, creating new occurrences of the entity or deleting them. These processes are recorded on the Entity Life History as process events, drawn as boxes the same shape as the entity box. These process event boxes show every event or process which can affect the entity over its lifetime. Some process events will access the entity for read only, some will update the entity, some will delete the occurrence altogether.

For example, the entity *invoice* contains all the details of all our invoices. Each occurrence must be created at some point. In our system, the invoice is created when the dispatch note is issued. We charge the customer as we send the goods. At this point the entity *invoice* has its birth event. Other events follow, such as a payment by a customer against the invoice or a query from the customer that puts the invoice into suspense. As a result of a query we may decide to issue a credit note against the invoice.

The use of the Entity Life History (ELH) is laid down in detail in the SSADM methodology. SSADM, however, is a methodology which is concerned with process analysis and design, not just data analysis and design. There is considerable debate among information systems professionals regarding the

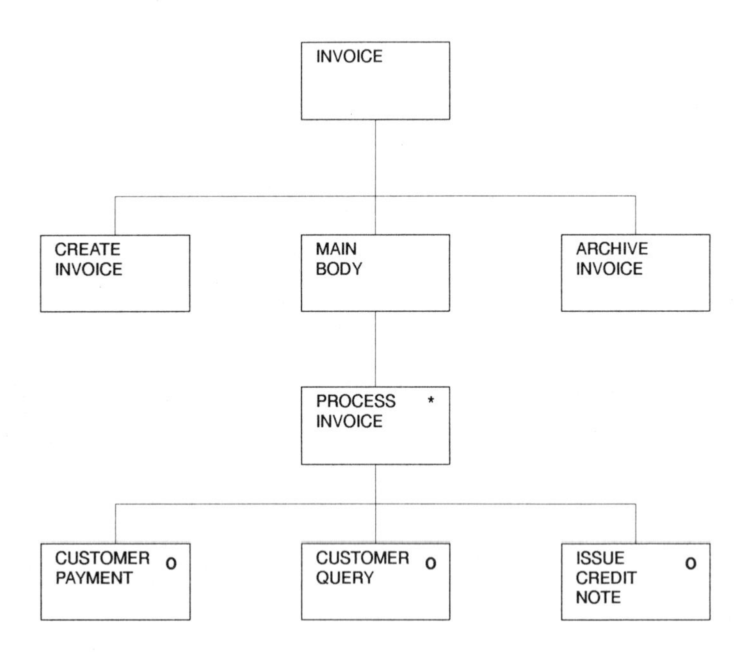

Figure 11-1 The Entity Life History: Invoice

process-data split in systems analysis and design. There are those that insist that data cannot be understood in isolation from the processes that operate upon it. There are others that argue that the data model is so fundamental to design that most process analysis is insignificant. This book is about data modelling, and does not pretend to be about process analysis and design. That being the case, how important are ELHs?

The ELH for many entities is very simple. The entity is created and it dies later. Various changes may be made to its attributes during its lifetime. To be thorough in our data analysis, we must look at these changes, so that we can verify that we have recorded all the entities and all the attributes of those entities.

If we are going to be thorough about our data analysis and design, we also need to know all those processes that change the status of the entity. For example, there may be an event that prints the invoices, ready for posting. This process may well update a flag or indicator attribute of the entity *invoice* to show that physical printing has taken place.

Nodes

A node is a box on the ELH which serves to improve the clarity of the ELH. It is not a process event but a logical point which normally has one or more process events below it. Nodes, although they are diagrammed with the same symbol — a rectangle — only exist to provide structure or organisation in the ELH. Processes can be identified by their position in the diagram, at the lowest level. All rectangles at the bottom of the hierachical structure are processes and all other rectangles are nodes.

In some data modelling approaches, the ELH contains only process events, but not nodes or the highest box for the entity. This may be because, using the SSADM rules, it is not always immediately clear to the untrained oberver which rectangles are events and which are not.

Sequence

The sequence of events in the ELH is strictly left to right. The process event at the extreme left is the birth event — the event at which an occurrence of the entity comes into existence. In the example shown the birth event is CREATE INVOICE. The process event at the extreme right is the death event — the point at which the occurrence of the entity is deleted. In the example shown, the death event is ARCHIVE INVOICE.

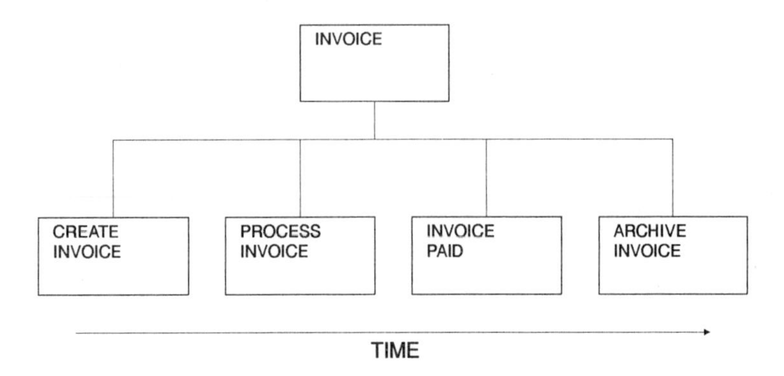

Figure 11-2 The Sequence of Nodes is Left to Right

There is a question as to whether the entity has been deleted at this point. Is the invoice in an archive file not still an invoice? It might be more accurate to show archiving as yet another process event, with the final deletion (after such time as the organisation deems appropriate) as the true death event.

This point reiterates the warning about keeping logical design separate from the physical details of implementation in a database. In a wholly logical design, *invoice* and *invoice-archive* (the entity in which *invoice* might be stored after archiving) would not appear as separate entities. The extent to which and the point at which each individual data analyst will introduce physical or implementation considerations varies, depending on the needs and circumstances of a project. The general rule, albeit meant to be broken if necessary, is: keep it logical.

Selection

A process event which has an 'O' or circle in the top right hand corner is one of a number of possible process events which may affect the entity at this point. Such processes are alternative events. For example, in the banking entity *customer-account*, the node TRANSACTION may consist of a number of alternative process events — cash paid in, direct credit, cash withdrawn, direct debit and standing order. All of these selections are possible events under the node TRANSACTION.

Iteration

A process event which has an asterisk (*) in the top right hand corner is a process event which can affect the entity many times from the same point in the structure of the ELH.

For example, in the banking world, an ELH for a customer account would probably show a birth event — the account creation, a death event — the closure of the account and an iterative process event — transaction. A transaction may occur an unlimited number of times, each transaction affecting the entity.

There are also other features which exist in the SSADM definition of the ELH which cater for yet more complex considerations.

Firstly, the concept of parallel structures is allowed for in SSADM, where a double horizontal line links process events which can occur concurrently or which do not have a predictable sequence.

Secondly, SSADM provides for the use of the 'quit and resume' mechanism — a kind of 'goto' command which allows the sequence of events to leap across the ELH in cases where the ELH has become very complex or unwieldy. While both of these mechanisms in SSADM have been developed to cater for situations which do occur, the data analyst will find them needed rarely, if at all.

Level of Design Detail

To produce a detailed ELH for every entity in the system would require a great deal of time. Do we want, or need, to be this thorough? This is not a question that should suggest a lack of professionalism or 'quick and dirty'. It is a very valid question. Quality is to do with giving the user what they need and what they want. To be overzealous in detail may not be to the user's advantage. The design of a data model for a large organisation may well be better carried out using evolutionary prototyping, and a first prototype would not be available within a short time span if full analysis and documentation of the kind described in SSADM occurred.

The time and effort involved in preparing detailed and validated ELHs for every entity in the system may exceed the benefits of doing so. However, the ELH is a well-defined and effective technique for charting the impact of processes on the entities of a system, and will certainly be used where appropriate by the experienced data analyst, especially in the case of complex or unclear entities or entities which are central to the operations of the organisation.

In systems development environments where SSADM has been specified as the systems development methodology ELHs are mandatory. Even when ELHs are not made mandatory, the data designer should produce them when to do so will improve the data analyst's understanding of the system or where the use of ELHs may allow improved communication between analyst and user.

ENTITY LIFE HISTORY

Summary

- An ELH (Entity Life History) is a diagram which shows all the events or processes in a system which affect an entity over the course of its life

  The entity appears as the highest box on the ELH

  A process event appears at the bottom of the diagram and has no boxes below it. All other boxes are nodes

  A node is not a process, and does not effect the entity. A node is shown to clarify the meaning of the ELH and has process events under it
- The sequence of the process events is strictly left to right on the diagram, except for
- Selection

  Process events with an 'O' or a circle in the top right hand corner are alternatives within the node above them

  and
- Iteration

  Process events with an asterisk (*) in the top right hand corner are iterative. The same process event or node can occur at the same point in the ELH
- Full use of ELHs may not be necessary in data modelling. ELHs are normally only prepared in data modelling where the entity is central to the organisation's operations or is particularly complex or unclear.

CASE STUDIES

In the following chapters two more case studies are explored in detail. There are a number of points which are applicable to the following two case studies, the case study already seen in Chapter 6 and to data modelling generally.

Firstly, these are case studies, not actual designs for real-world database structures. They have been designed to illustrate the techniques and issues of data modelling. For this reason, some aspects of the case studies have been kept as simple as possible to make them easier to understand. Other aspects have been examined in great detail, with the intention of exploring some of the more subtle and complex issues in data modelling. Given the very limited information upon which these case studies are based, many possible solutions exist. In a real world data modelling exercise, the team of data analysts would have access to a mass of interview records, and a much wider range of business documents. They should also have the benefit of access to key users in order to clarify questions raised during analysis and the preparation of the data model. If the reader or the analyst makes slightly different assumptions than those in the text, the model will differ.

It has been said that if a hundred data analysts are asked to supply a working model for the same requirement, a hundred different solutions are quite likely, all workable, all subtly different. There is never a single correct model for any information environment.

Secondly, the case study discussions are meant to illustrate the way of thinking of the good data analyst. It is not intended that these case studies should cover all possible discussions, but many interesting possibilities have been explored. A good data analyst will possess both an enquiring mind and an instinct to ask that one last question and examine that one last possibility.

The notes at the end of each case study chapter may be omitted on the first reading.

CHAPTER 12

JACK GOLD MUSICAL AGENT

General Information

Jack Gold is a highly successful musical agent who has contracts with many top international bands and performers. He has placed acts at such renowned venues as Wembley Stadium, Wembley Arena, The Marquee and the NEC. Jack has a contract with every act, detailing performance conditions, penalties, fees and Jack's percentage. Jack's contracts are always with the act — whether it is a limited company or only a collection of individuals, and every individual artist signs the contract. Contracts are usually renewed annually, and Jack keeps records of past contracts.

Jack wants to record each performance including information on the date, time and venue of the performance, the house (number in the audience) and the fee. Jack always pays each act one fee for one performance and insists that this must remain so. Fees can be paid in several instalments and a payment can sometimes cover a number of fees.

The managers of bands or acts will usually provide technicians, roadies, drivers, sound and lighting staff and other staff needs, but Jack can supply these from his own stables. He pays his support staff one fee for one performance, too. Bands will often play support for other bands, but in these cases the performances are treated as separate from each other.

Discussion

There are a number of easily identifiable entities in the explanations given in the general introduction section. Bands, performers, acts and artists all sound similar, and may be synonyms. This will need to be clarified. A venue is a very clear entity: it has a name which uniquely identifies it, it has other attributes - its address, its size and so on. Is it of interest to the business? Ask Jack. 'Oh, most certainly', says Jack. 'We need to know which venues bands are booked at.'

'By the way, Jack, what is the difference between these things:

- Group
- Band
- Artist
- Act
- Performer ?'

'Well, a group and a band are the same thing, I think', says Jack. 'An artist is a person, the same thing as a performer. An act is either a person or a group of people.' 'Ah,' says the analyst, 'would it be true to say:

```
An act must have at least one person (the
artist) in it, but an artist must belong to one
and only one act?'
```

This would give us a one-to-many relationship between *act* and *artist*. The ERM for this would appear as in Figure 12-1.

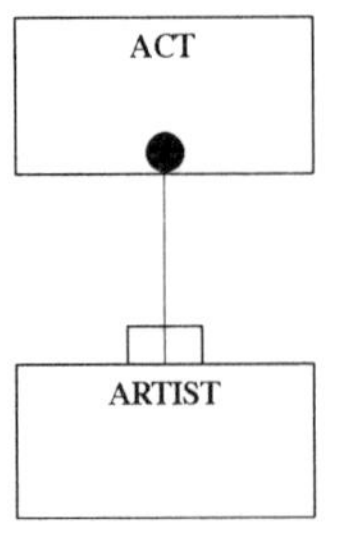

Figure 12-1 The ERM for One-To-Many: Act and Artist

An act must have at least one and may have many artists associated with it, but an artist must belong to one and only one act.

Figure 12-2 The ERM for Many-To-Many: Act and Artist

Discussing the business with the user, we discover that:
An act can have many artists in it and an artist can be in many acts.

'That sounds about right', replies Jack, 'except that an artist can be in several different acts.'

'I see', says the analyst, 'then it would it be better to say:

```
An act must have at least one artist in it and
may have many artists in it, and an artist must
belong to at least one act and may belong to
many acts?'
```

'Right!' says Jack. 'That is exactly it.'

We have a many-to-many relationship between *act* and *artist* which must be decomposed (see Figures 12-2 and 12-3).

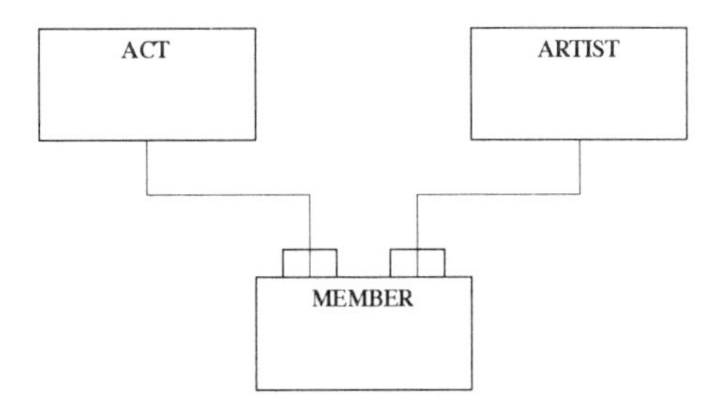

Figure 12-3 Act and Artist and Their Link Entity

The many-to-many between act and artist has been decomposed, using the link entity member.

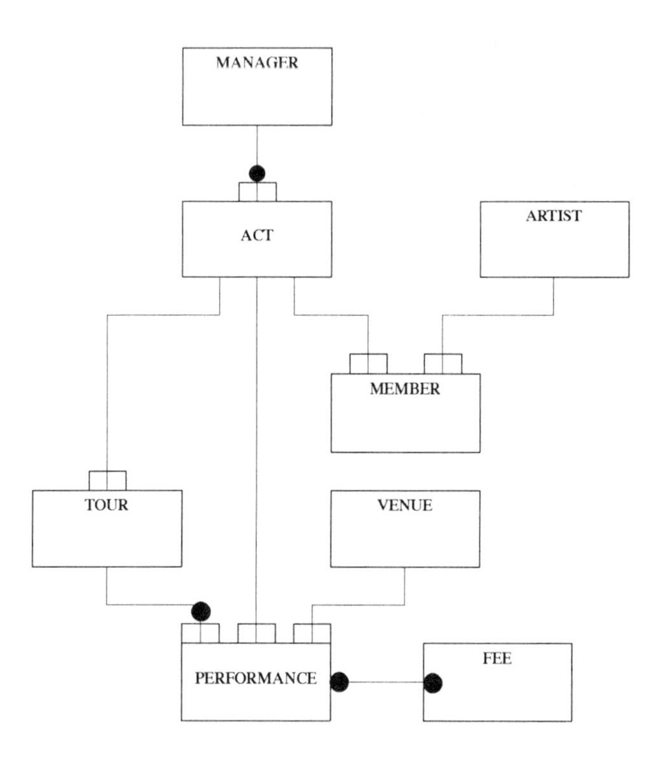

Figure 12-4 The Final ERM For Jack Gold

In this ERM, only those memberships which do not adhere to Type C have been marked, showing where special action needs to be taken in the implementation. See the discussion and the notes in this case study for an explanation of each. See the chapters on one-to-one and ERM advanced topics for explanations on the marking of one-to-one and non-default memberships.

Relationship Rules

The following rules have now been agreed with Jack, and although some of them are somewhat restrictive, Jack has agreed to the design within these rules. A number of them are questionable, and are discussed in the notes at the end of this case study.

> A manager may manage zero, one or many acts, and an act may have zero or one and only one manager.
>
> An act must have at least one and may have many artists in it, and an artist must belong to one and may belong to many acts.
>
> An act may have zero, one or many performances, but a performance must be by one and only one act.
>
> An act may have zero, one or many tours, but a tour must relate to one and only one act.
>
> A venue may host zero, one or many performances, but a performance must occur at one and only one venue.
>
> A tour may be composed of zero, one or many performances, and a performance may be part of zero, or one and only one tour.
>
> A performance will result in one and only one fee and a fee must relate to one and only one performance.

Let us look at the ERM for Jack's business (see Figure12-4).

Data Tables

Manager(Manager-Code, Manager-Name, Manager-Address, Status, Rating)

Act(Act-Name, Music-Type-Code, Grade, Average-Earnings, Manager-Code)

Artist(Artist-Number, Artist-Name, Artist-Address, Date-Of-Birth)

Member(Act-Name, Artist-Number)

Tour(Tour-Name, Tour-Description, Start-Date, Act-Name)

Performance(Act-Name, Date-Of-Performance, Time-Of-Performance, House, Time-Start, On-Stage-Time, Cash-Takings, Tour-Name, Venue-Name)

Venue(Venue-Name, Capacity, Location-Address, Contact-Name, Telephone-Number)

Fee(Act-Name, Date-Of-Performance, Time-Of-Performance, Amount, Amount-Paid, Transaction-Number)

CREATE Statements

The SQL create statements for the tables defined in the previous section have been included here to demonstrate the simple step from tables to create statements. Where the tables are simple lists of the attributes of an entity, with the unique identifier and foreign keys underlined, the create statements are actual SQL statements which instruct the database management system to build the data files to hold the data. The data analyst must at this stage specify the type and size of each item of data, thereby instructing the database management system to build the files with these storage spaces to hold the data. The task of determining size and type of the item is the analyst's and can usually be dealt with by examining the documents from which the original analysis was done.

```
Create Table MANAGER
        (Manager_Code           Char(3) not null,
        Manager_Surname         Char(20),
        Manager_Initials        Char(4),
        Manager_Address_1       Char(30),
        Manager_Address_2       Char(30),
        Manager_Address_3       Char(30),
        Manager_Postcode        Char(10),
```

```
        Status_Code             Char(1),
        Rating_Code             Char(1));

Create Table ACT
        (Act_Name               Char(12) not null,
        Music_Type_Code         Char(2),
        Grade                   Char(4),
        Average_Earnings        Number(6),
        Manager_Code            Char(3));

Create Table ARTIST
        (Artist_Number          Char(12) not null,
        Artist_Surname          Char(20),
        Artist_First_Name       Char(12),
        Artist_Address_1        Char(30),
        Artist_Address_2        Char(30),
        Artist_Address_3        Char(30),
        Artist_Postcode         Char(10),
        Date_Of_Birth           Date);

Create Table MEMBER
        (Act_Name               Char(12) not null,
        Artist_Number           Char(12) not null);

Create Table TOUR
        (Tour_Name              Char(12) not null,
        Tour_Description        Char(30),
        Start_Date              Date,
        Act_Name                Char(12));

Create Table PERFORMANCE
        (Act_Name               Char(12) not null,
        Date_Of_Performance     Date   not null,
        Time_Of_Performance     Number(4) not null,
        House                   Number(6),
        Time_Start              Number(4),
        On_Stage_Time           Number(4),
        Cash_Takings            Number(6,)
        Tour-Name               Char(12),
        Venue_Name              Char(12));
```

```
Create Table VENUE
        Venue_Name              Char(12) not null,
        Capacity                Number(7),
        Location_Address_1      Char(30),
        Location_Address_2      Char(30),
        Location_Address_3      Char(30),
        Contact_Name            Char(30),
        Telephone_Number        Char(12));

Create Table FEE
        (Act_Name               Char(12) not null,
        Date_Of_Performance     Date  not null,
        Time_Of_Performance     Number(4) not null,
        Amount                  Number(6),
        Amount_Paid             Number(6),
        Transaction_Number      Char(13));
```

Some of the data names in the above CREATE statements differ from the names specified in the data tables. When implementing the data tables designed by the analyst into actual data definition statements in the database management system, it is permissible to make changes to the names of the data items or tables and is usual to split items into their natural sub-divisions.

The changes may be desirable for a number of reasons. Firstly, items which were treated as a single item by the data analyst during the analysis of the *structure* of the data model, such as Manager-Name, can be split into separate items in the database, such as Manager-Surname and Manager-Initials. If this is done, the items may then be retrieved separately and in whichever order is desired. On an alphabetical report, for example, it may be preferable to list the surname, followed by the initials, but when addressing a letter, it would be better to have the initials followed by the surname.

The address itself has been split into multiple lines, to allow the lines to be printed one after another. Other changes exist to improve clarity, eliminate confusion and to facilitate flexible retrieval and output.

Notes

1. Jack explains that the transaction-number (in the table *fee*) is a number, not a character item as is shown in the table. Much of the interaction between data analyst and user is a two-way education process. The user is educating the analyst in how the business works and the analyst is educating the user

in data analysis and database design. The explanation to Jack of the transaction-number data type might be as follows:

> The computer stores items according to how they are used. Numeric values are stored as numbers so that they can have mathematical operations carried out on them — so they can be added together, subtracted or averaged, for example. Although the transaction-number is composed of *numeric characters*, they will never need to be added together or averaged. They are not so much *numbers* as *codes*.

It is simpler and more correct to store numeric *codes* as character items. For validation, we could tell the dictionary that only numeric characters are permitted in this data item.

2. The closed area, bounded by the relationships between *performance*, *tour* and *act*, has come about because of a chasm trap. There is no doubt that we must be able to establish the link between *act* and *performance* — it is, after all, the act that does the performance. If we were to establish the link through *tour*, then we could enquire of the database,

> which tours have such-and-such an act been on, and which performances are associated with these tours?

You will note, however, that for the entity *performance*, the membership of the *tour-performance* relationship is optional. That is to say:

```
A tour may have zero, one or many performances,
and a performance may be associated with either
zero, or one and only one tour.
```

For this reason, any performances which were not part of a *tour* could not be linked to *act*, if the only relationship between *act* and *performance* was through *tour*. It is for this reason that we need to create a direct link between *performance* and *act*. This extra relationship, between *act* and *performance* directly, guarantees that we will always be able to establish which performances were by which acts, whether they were part of a tour or not.

This is an example of the bypass solution to the chasm trap. The alternative solution is to set up a dummy occurrence of *tour* called 'none', and then associate all non-tour performances with it. This would be an example of the override solution to the chasm trap.

3. There is a one-to-one relationship between *performance* and *fee*. This is because, during our discussions with the user, Jack explicitly stated that this must be the case. It is the way he runs his business, and the data model must reflect the user's wishes, especially when the user is insistent.

You will notice that both ends of the one to one have been membership marked. This is because one-to-one relationships cannot be identified with any one of the four combinations of membership, of which type C is the default. Thus, it is advisable to explicitly mark them. In this case, the relationship rule is:

```
A performance will result in one and only one
fee and a fee must relate to one and only one
performance.
```

The word must is the give-away, and identifies a mandatory membership.

The *fee* must have a *performance*. The membership is therefore marked as mandatory by placing a membership marker inside the *fee* entity rectangle, next to the relationship line. At the other end of the line, the membership is optional. A *performance* does not have to have a *fee*, either because the performance is a charity performance or because the performance may be recorded in the database before *fee* has been paid.

In the data tables, you will notice that the key of *performance* has been embedded in the *fee* table, because if a *fee* exists, we must establish the relationship to *performance*, which must already exist. The key of *fee* should not be stored in *performance*, because when the performance is stored in the database, *fee* may not yet exist. We would have wasted space.

4. Jack has agreed with the relationship rules that are listed earlier, and will work with them, although he has some doubts. Jack is not sure, for example, about the rule that an *act* can have many *tours*, but that a *tour* can only relate to one *act*. Is it not true, thinks Jack, that several *acts* can be on one *tour*? The rule that an *act* can only have one *manager*, is also questionable. Over a period of time, an act may have many managers. Both of these objections are reasonable, and the model could be changed to accommodate the different rules. However, for the sake of simplicity, not all business rules are always implemented in a data model for a real organisation. Sometimes, compromises have to be made. For the purposes of this implementation of Jack's database, we are then only recording the current manager, and we are treating

two different acts touring together as two concurrent tours. Jack can live with this.

CHAPTER 13

L & I SHIPPING COMPANY

General information

London and Ireland Shipping Company PLC (LISC) was founded in 1952 and owns several fleets of ships for cargo use only. The company has historically run passenger lines, but recent policy decisions involved the sale of all passenger-carrying vessels. The line currently has 14 vessels, including one tanker and one tug-boat operating out of Liverpool. Most of the vessels are registered in Liberia for tax reasons.

Each ship has one or more holds divided into spaces. These spaces are defined by steel bulkheads or other physical barriers, which define a measured volume. Sister ships, built by the same shipbuilders and to the same designs have similar names, such as *Pride of Ireland*, *Queen of Ireland*, *Song of Ireland* and *Warrior of Ireland*. Sister ships have identical cargo storage facilities except where they have been modified since their launching.

Contracts are taken out with agents for one or more manifests (lists of cargo items to be shipped). The kinds of cargo typically carried by LISC include grain, coal and ores (carried only in ships equipped with bulk cargo holds), sacked grain, heavy cases, containers (which may be carried on deck), pallets and so on.

Cargo items may take up less than one space in a hold, or one or more spaces, depending on the size of the item. A space may therefore contain several small cargo items.

The ships of the LISC are kept as busy and as full as possible, in order to maximise the investment in vessels and minimise running costs. LISC's ships ply most of the seas of the world, but tend to operate mainly in the Mediterranean, the North and Mid Atlantic and the Indian Ocean. Different ships require different crew complements. Even sister ships may have slightly different crew rosters.

The owners wish to keep records of their employees and the ships they are assigned to, as well as the sailings of their ships with the start and end ports.

LISC intends to use the system for producing invoices for agents and customers, and will want the new system to produce a data transfer file for interfacing with the existing accounting / invoicing system. LISC also wishes to use the system to analyse the efficiency of use of cargo space and of percentage wasted cargo space for ships on legs and voyages.

Following discussions with the owners the scope diagram (zero level DFD) has been produced and agreed. (See Figure 13-1.)

Discussion

There are a number of very strong entities in the information given. A ship is a physical thing, central to the system, uniquely identifiable by either the name of the ship or the registration number. We will use the registration number, because it has a fixed length, as opposed to the ship's name, which may be quite long and composed of characters and spaces. What might the table for the entity *ship* look like?

Ship(Registration-number, Name, Tonnage, Length, Draft,
Beam, Date-Of-Registration)

We ask the owners: do you wish to store details of crew members and the current or historical (i.e. past) duties? The owners are clear on this, they would like to know who is on which ship, so that pay details can be sent to captains. For audit purposes, we also need to keep the historical details for two years after the period of duty.

We have another clear entity: *crew-member* or, for brevity, *crew*. What would the table for *crew* look like?

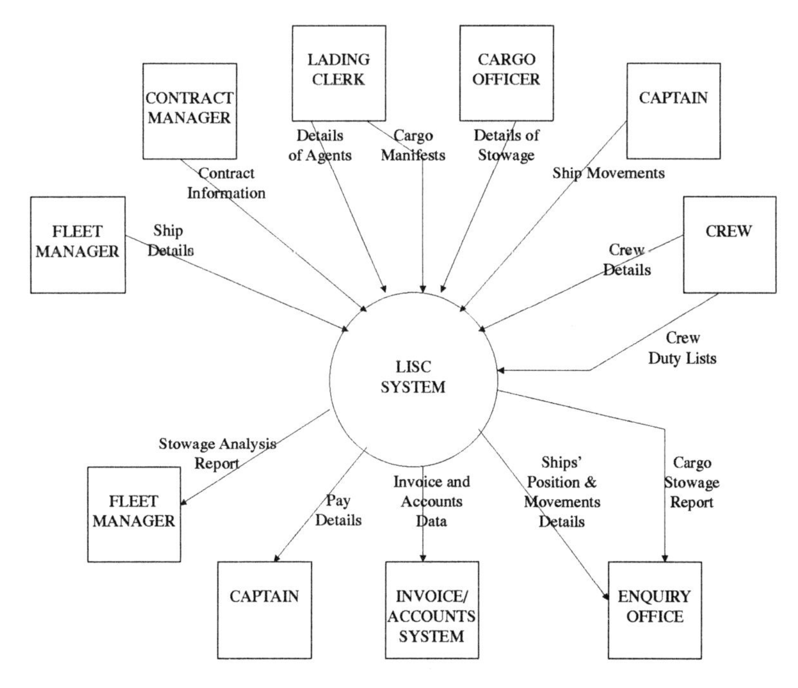

Figure 13-1 The LISC Scope Diagram

The Scope Diagram, or Zero Level DFD, shows all inputs and outputs from the system, which originate from or are recieved by the external entities.

Crew(<u>Crew-N-I-Number</u>, Surname, Initials, Date-Started, Grade, Duty, Ship-Registration-Number, Pay-Rate,Pay-Number, Bank-Details)

If the information about which ship the crew member is on is to be historical, surely there may be more than one Ship-Registration-Number for a crew member? This is then a repeating item or group, and has to be removed from the crew table. What is the relationship rule for the relationship between *crew* and *ship*?

```
Over a period of time, a crew member may be
assigned to many ships, and a ship may have
many crew members associated with it.
```

Figure 13-2 Many-To-Many: Crew and Ship

What does the ERM for this system look like at this point in the analysis? We now have a many-to-many relationship between CREW and SHIP (see Figure 13-2).

This relationship has to be decomposed. A link entity has to be created to hold the occurrences of the relationship between *crew* and *ship*. Let us call it *duty* (see Figure 13-3).

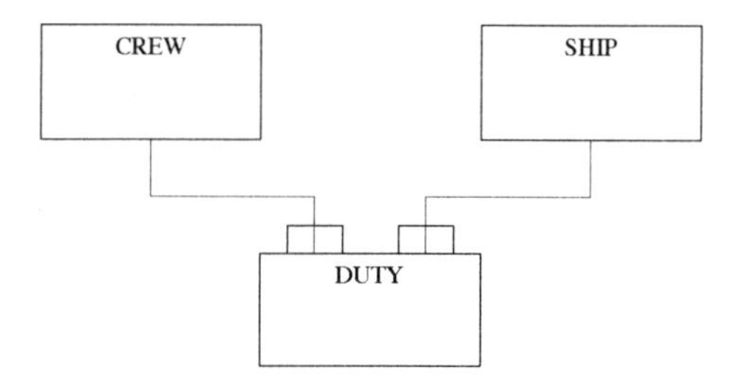

Figure 13-3 Crew and Ship Linked By Duty

What other things which may be entities are there in the documents that have been supplied? Agent is a person, or a company, and therefore unique — it is certainly of interest to the system. Agents sign contracts. Contracts result in manifests. Contracts and manifests are both unique, both identifiable, both of interest.

On the manifest document, we see that ships have named holds, and holds have numbered spaces. The owners confirm that these terms are important.

On the ship movements document, we discover that a ship has an identifiable and unique voyage, which is made up of several trips from port to port. The term sailing is a synonym for voyage, and discussions with the users reveals that they would prefer the term *sailing* as the entity-name. The owners confirm that the trips from port to port are called legs, that a sailing is made of legs, that a leg is between two ports. Are leg and port entities? Certainly. The only way to identify a leg is as part of a sailing and between two ports. *leg*, *sailing* and *port* are unique, identifiable and of interest. *Port* is a place entity. *Leg* and *sailing* are event entities.

We are now in a position to consider the relationship rules in detail.

Relationship Rules

The following relationship rules describe in English-like sentences the relationships between the entities in the final ERM for LISC. These rules may be explained to the users, who will then confirm or refute their truth in the context of their business and the system that they want.

> A fleet may contain zero, one or many ships, but a ship must be part of one and only one fleet.
>
> A ship-type may apply to zero, one or many ships, but a ship must be of one and only one ship-type.
>
> A ship may have zero, one or many duty records (about crew assignments), but a duty record must belong to one and only one ship.
>
> A crew member may have zero, one or many duty records (about ship assignments), but a duty record must belong to one and only one crew member.
>
> An agent may be associated with zero, one or many contracts, but a contract must be with one and only one agent.
>
> A contract may result in zero, one or many manifests, but a manifest must be associated with one and only one contract.

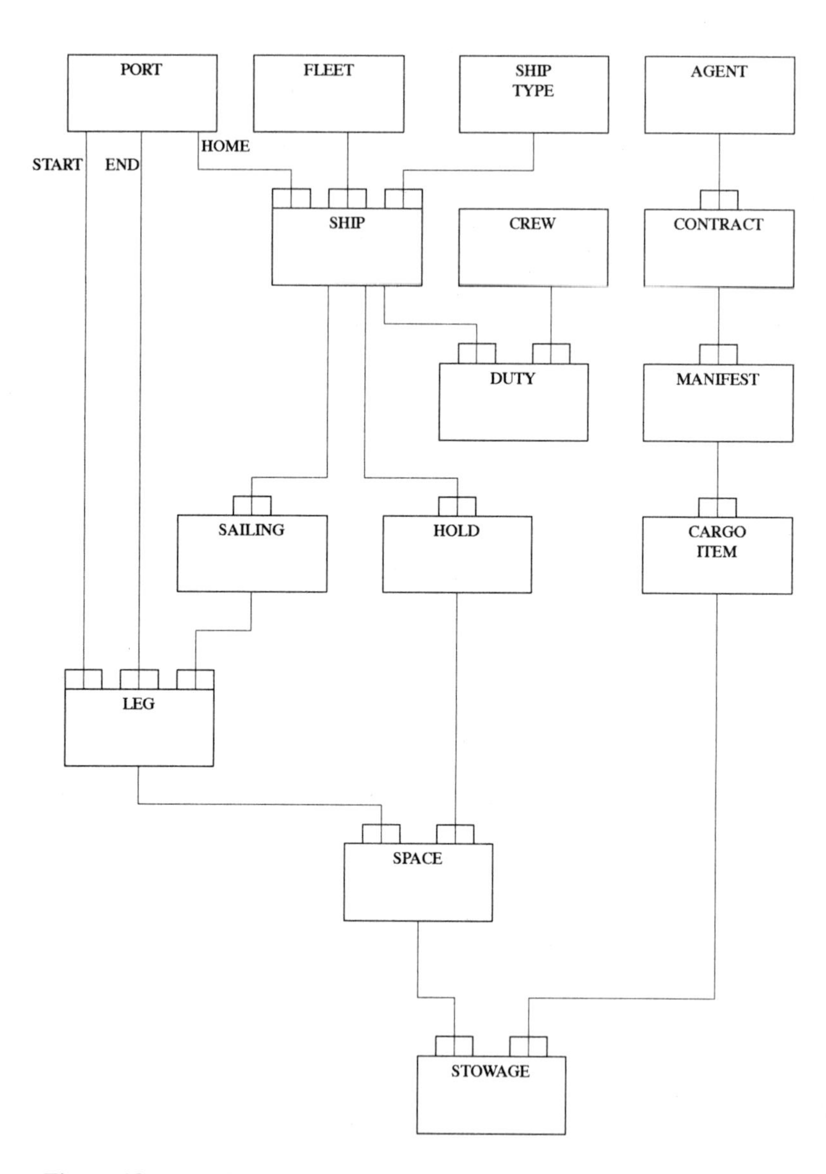

Figure 13-4 The Final ERM for L & I Shipping

A manifest may have zero, one or many cargo items on it, but an item of cargo must be on one and only one manifest.

A ship may have zero, one or many holds, but a hold must be in one and only one ship.

A hold may have zero, one or many spaces, but a space must be in one and only one hold.

A ship may have zero, one or many sailings, but a sailing relates to one and only one ship.

A sailing may have zero, one or many legs, but a leg must be a part of one and only one sailing.

A port may be associated with zero, one or many legs as start port or end port, and a leg must be associated with two and only two ports (one the start port and one the end port).

A port may be the home port to many different ships, but a ship must have one and only one home port.

A hold may be divided into zero, one or many spaces *for each leg* but a space *for each leg* must be associated with one and only one hold.

A leg may be associated with zero, one or many spaces, but a space must be associated with one and only one leg.

A space may contain zero, one or many cargo items, and a cargo item may be stored in one or many spaces.

The last rule given has been left in the many-to-many form, because the English for the decomposed relationships is very obscure. On the diagram, however, you can see that the many-to-many relationship between *space* and *cargo-item* has been resolved by the use of the link entity *stowage*. The entity *stowage* holds the information about which cargo-item is in which space on which leg of which sailing.

Data Tables

Ship-Type(Ship-Type-Code, Description)

Fleet(Fleet-Code, Fleet Name)

Agent(Agent-Reference, Name, Address, Telephone, Contact, Status)

Contract(Contract-Number, Terms, Agent-Reference, Conditions, Date-Of-Contract, Status)

Ship(Ship-Registration, Tonnage, Home-Port-Code, Country-Of-Registration, Beam, Draft, Ship-Type-Code, Fleet-Code, Date-Built)

Crew(Crew-N-I-Number,Surname, Initials, Date-Started, Grade, Pay-Number, Bank-Details)

Hold(Ship-Registration, Hold-Name, Width, Depth, Height, Capacity, Type)

Duty(Ship-Registration,Crew-N-I-Number, Date-Commenced, Date-Finished, Position)

Manifest(Manifest-Number, Contract-Number, Date-Of-Manifest)

Port(Port-Code, Port-Name, Latitude, Longitude, Facilities, Harbour-Depth)

Sailing(Ship-Registration, Date-Of-Sailing)

Leg(Ship-Registration, Date-Of-Sailing, Start-Port-Code, End-Port-Code)

Space(Ship-Registration, Date-Of Sailing, Start-Port-Code, End-Port-Code, Hold-Name, Space-Number, Capacity)

Cargo-Item(Manifest-Number, Item-Number, Description)

Stowage(Ship-Registration, Date-Of Sailing, Start-Port-Code, End-Port-Code, Hold-Name, Space-Number, Manifest-Number, Item-Number)

CREATE Statements

```
Create Table SHIP_TYPE
        (Ship_Type_Code    Char(2)  not null,
        Description        Char(20));

Create Table FLEET
        (Fleet_Code        Char(2)  not null,
        Fleet_Name         Char(15));

Create Table AGENT
        (Agent_Reference   Char(6)  not null,
        Agent_Name         Char(30),
        Agent_Address_1    Char(30),
        Agent_Address_2    Char(30),
        Agent_Address_3    Char(30),
        Agent_Telephone    Char(12),
        Contact            Char(20),
        Status             Char(2));

Create Table CONTRACT
        (Contract_Number   Char(8)  not null,
        Terms              Char(20),
        Agent_Reference    Char(6),
        Conditions         Char(20),
        Date_Of_Contract   Date,
        Status             Char(2));

Create Table SHIP
        (Ship_Registration Char(6)  not null,
        Tonnage            Number(5),
        Home_Port_Code     Char(4),
        Country_Of_Reg     Char(7),
        Beam               Number(7),
        Draft              Number(7),
```

```
                Ship_Type_Code      Char(2),
                Fleet_Code          Char(2),
                Date_Built          Date);

Create Table CREW
                (Crew_N_I_Number Char(12)  not null,
                Crew_Surname        Char(30),
                Crew_Initials       Char(7),
                Date_Started        Date,
                Grade               Char(2),
                Pay_Number          Char(8),
                Bank_Sort_Code      Char(6),
                Bank_Account_No     Char(8));

Create Table HOLD
                (Ship_Registration  Char(6)  not null,
                Hold_Name_Code      Char(1)  not null,
                Width               Number(7,2),
                Depth               Number(7,2),
                Height              Number(7,2),
                Capacity            Number(6,2),
                Type                Char(2));

Create Table DUTY
                (Ship_Registration  Char(6)  not null,
                Crew_N_I_Number     Char(12) not null,
                Date_Commenced      Date   not null,
                Date_Finished       Date,
                Position            Char(40));

Create Table  MANIFEST
                (Manifest_Number    Char(15) not null,
                Contract_Number     Char(8),
                Date_Of_Manifest    Date);

Create Table PORT
                (Port_Code          Char(4)  not null,
                Port_Name           Char(20),
                Latitude            Number(3),
                Longitude           Number(3),
                Facilities          Char(40),
                Harbour_Depth       Number(3));
```

```
Create Table SAILING
              (Ship_Registration   Char(6) not null
              Date_Of_Sailing      Date   not null);

Create Table LEG
              (Ship_Registration   Char(6) not null,
              Date_Of_Sailing      Date   not null,
              Start_Port_Code      Char(4) not null,
              End_Port_Code        Char(4) not null);

Create Table SPACE
              (Ship_Registration   Char(6) not null,
              Date_Of_Sailing      Date   not null,
              Start_Port_Code      Char(4) not null,
              End_Port_Code        Char(4) not null,
              Hold_Name_Code       Char(1) not null,
              Space_Number         Char(3) not null,
              Capacity             Number(4));

Create Table CARGO_ITEM
              (Manifest_Number     Char(15)  not null,
              Item_Number          Char(3)  not null,
              Description          Char(50));

Create Table STOWAGE
              (Ship_Registration   Char(6) not null,
              Date_Of_Sailing      Date   not null,
              Start_Port_Code      Char(4) not null,
              End_Port_Code        Char(4) not null,
              Hold_Name_Code       Char(1) not null,
              Space_Number         Char(3) not null,
              Manifest_Number      Char(15)  not null,
              Item_Number          Char(3) not null);
```

Notes

1. In the final ERM for LISC, there is a closed area, bounded by the relationships between *ship*, *hold*, *sailing*, *leg* and *space*. This is caused by the need to associate space with leg. A *space* is a physical location, but the same space may be used to store different cargo items on different legs of the

sailing. With the model as shown in the final ERM, an enquiry of the database could determine which numbered cargo item was located in which *space* during which *leg*. Each physical *space*, you could say, has many logical spaces over many legs of many sailings.

Indeed, the model could be changed to show *space* distinct from the space on a particular leg. This would have the advantage of keeping a permanent record of the physical spaces in a ship's hold, independently of their use on different legs. Each physical space would then have a many-to-many relationship with *leg*, and would then be decomposed into a link entity called *space-leg*. It then would be the *space-leg* entity which is associated with *stowage*. (See Figure 13-5.)

2. The unique identifiers for some of the tables may be clarified with some further explanation. The table *hold* has a unique identifier which is the concatenation of the *ship* reference and the hold name. This is because the hold name repeats for each *ship* and is not unique on its own. For example, *Pride of Ireland* and *Song of Ireland* both have forward and stern holds, a deck (which the owners think of as a kind of hold)and so on. Only by putting the two items together do we have a unique identifier.

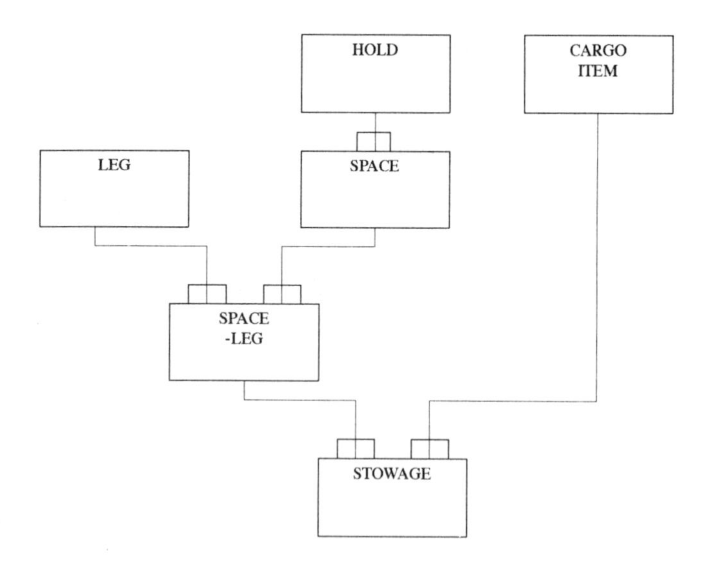

Figure 13-5 A Possible Variation on the LISC ERM

In the case of object oriented databases, no unique identifier is considered necessary. Both items are needed to locate the correct record, but as long as they can both be accessed, and as long as the record can be retrieved using both keys, there is really no need for a single key to be formed.

The unique identifier for the table *duty* is formed from the keys of both parent entities plus the date of commencement of the period of duty. These three items uniquely identify the record. The date of commencement of the period of duty is necessary because the crew member could have two distinct periods of duty on the same ship. In this case, the identifiers for *ship* and *crew* alone would not be sufficient to uniquely identify the record.

The unique identifier of the entity *stowage* is composed of the keys of both parent entities, with no other attributes. It is therefore a true link entity. The fact that both parent entities already have concatenated keys makes the key very long. There is an argument for a system-generated key to be the unique identifier, to improve performance.

3. *Hold* and *space* information, if identical for all vessels of the same type, could be linked to *ship-type*, rather than the vessel itself. This would avoid duplication, and would be more elegant. In some situations, such a strategy would be a great improvement.

Consider the seating arrangement on an airliner. All 747 jets, if they have the same seating structure, would not have to have their own seating structure defined, but would inherit this information from the *aircraft-type* entity (a classification entity). The actual seats to be booked would be a seat from the aircraft-type linked to the aircraft and/or the flight.

In the case of LISC, however, the information given states that the stowage facilities vary even within the same type of ship, due to modifications since launching. Therefore, in this case, we must store *hold* and *space* information for each vessel individually.

4. *Port* and *duty* have not been associated on the final ERM for the business. The owners, confirm, however, that periods of duty always begin and end at a port. There have been rare cases of crew members being taken off ships by helicopter for emergency medical treatment, but these are exceptional situations. Following a discussion with the owners about whether they need to know the port at which a period of duty starts or ends, it was decided not to create a relationship between the entities *duty* and *port*. Since we know the

ship and the start and end dates for any period of duty, and we know the ship and the start and end dates for any sailing, we can work out the same information from data already held in the model.

<table>
<tr><td colspan="3">Ship Movements</td></tr>
<tr><td colspan="3">SS Pride of Ireland

33000 tonnes Type R Vessel Cargo
Fleet: Far East</td></tr>
<tr><td>Registration Number
188937783</td><td colspan="2">Captain
T. Harmon
775665</td></tr>
<tr><td colspan="3">Sailing :London-Delhi (27/5/90-14/7/90)</td></tr>
<tr><td>Port Of Call</td><td>Date Arrive</td><td>Date Sailed</td></tr>
<tr><td>London</td><td></td><td>30.5.90</td></tr>
<tr><td>Rotterdam</td><td>1.6.90</td><td>2.6.90</td></tr>
<tr><td>Oporto</td><td>7.6.90</td><td>10.6.90</td></tr>
<tr><td>Suez</td><td>17.6.90</td><td>20.6.90</td></tr>
<tr><td>Delhi</td><td>14.7.90</td><td></td></tr>
</table>

Figure 13-6 The Ship Movements Document

Manifest 7892348234/AS Page 17

Agent R.S.Thompson 10 Timberwell St Easthampton

Shipped on : *Pride of Ireland* Voyage London-Delhi 27/5/90

Item No		Hold	Space
38	Machine Parts Case Numbered 08914	Forward	25
39	Machine Parts Case Numbered 98235	Forward	25
40	Oil, Drum 100 litres 200 of	Deck Cargo	10,11,17
41	Bearings, Ball, 10mm,Case Numbered 892955	Forward	
42	Generator, Electrical/Diesel Serial 9828FG762	Stern	55
43	Diesel Fuel, Drum 100 litres 60 of	Stern	17,22,23

Figure 13-7 The Manifest Document

CHAPTER 14

DEVELOPING DATABASE APPLICATIONS

☐ **Data Modelling During Development — Waterfall Approach compared with The Iterative Approach — The involvement of Data Analysis and the Data Analyst — Feasibility — Analysis and Design — First Prototype — Iterative Development — Commissioning and the Evolution of the System**

Data Modelling During Development

In this chapter, we will be looking at the role of the data analyst and practical data modelling in the development of database applications. Traditionally, the systems analyst and the data analyst have been involved in the systems development life cycle only during the analysis and design phases.

However, the data analyst can and should contribute to the development of both new and existing systems at other points in the process. Furthermore, practical data modelling skills are a very useful adjunct to other systems development skills and can be very effectively employed during other phases and during other elements in the systems building process.

Waterfall Approach

There are thought to be two fundamental approaches to the building of computer information systems. These are the *waterfall* approach and the *iterative* approach. The waterfall approach is composed of a number of steps which follow on from each other in a sequence (see Figure 14-1). The waterfall approach, as its name suggests, has the characteristic of not being able to go back through the steps. Once a step is complete, it is fixed and the process of development must move on to the next step. No review or modification of previous steps or their results is permitted. In the same way as water cannot flow back up the waterfall, nor can the process of development go back even one step.

This has both advantages and disadvantages. The advantage of the waterfall approach is that it easy to manage and plan, because exact and unalterable

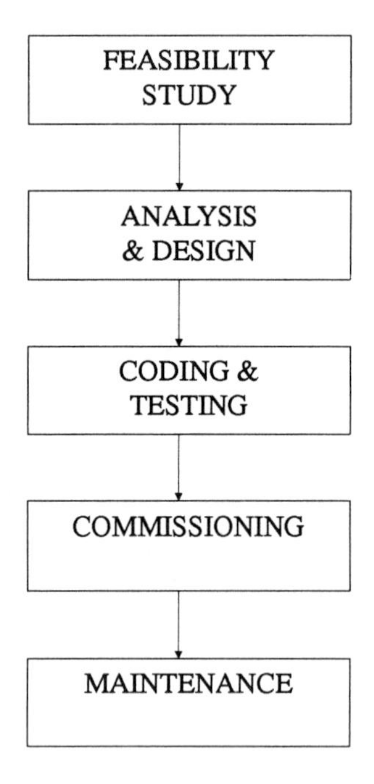

Figure 14-1 Waterfall Systems Development

In the classic waterfall approach to building computer systems each step happens after the completion of the last and more importantly, the development cannot return to a previous step once it is complete.

dates can be set as milestones in the project. This means that development staff are quite clear on where they are in the development process and the various tasks which must be carried out in each phase are clear-cut. The problem with the waterfall approach is that if errors, omissions or misunderstandings occur at any stage of the project and are not addressed or corrected during that phase, they cannot be rectified until the system is delivered and installed. At this point, maintenance may begin. Maintenance of systems built using the waterfall approach normally starts with correcting errors of speci-

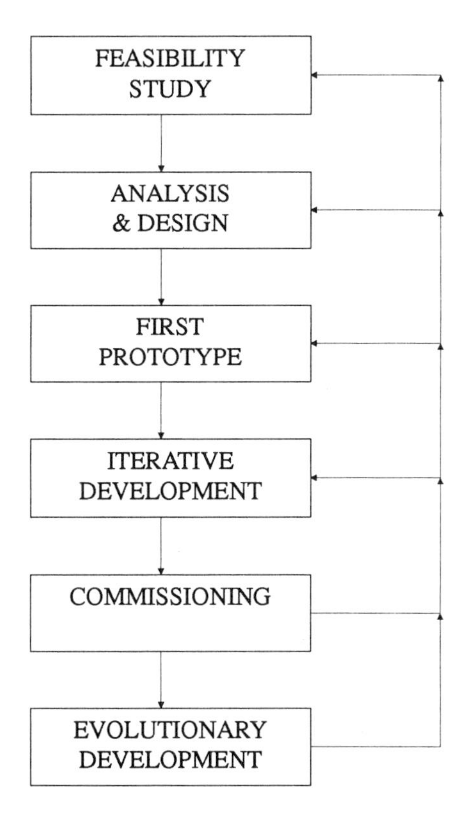

Figure 14-2 Iterative Systems Development

In the Iterative Approach, the development team can revisit any phase of development at any time, to improve or correct the result of that phase. Iterative development is also characterised by high levels of user input to the development process.

fication, design or coding which came about during the development process.

The waterfall approach makes the rather unwarranted assumption that the processes and techniques employed at each stage will correctly identify user needs, will produce the correct design to satisfy these needs and will correctly implement the design. It is the experience of most systems developers that none of these assumptions is reasonable, and for this reason the second of our fundamental approaches, the iterative approach, is increasingly advocated for use with information systems development. These two approaches are sometimes referred to a conservative and radical. Most systems development projects inevitably use not one approach or the other, but a mixture of both.

Iterative Approach

The iterative approach follows much the same sequence of phases as the waterfall approach. After all, in both cases, the same basic tasks need to be carried out. The iterative approach differs from the waterfall approach in that it is assumed that errors, omissions and misconceptions will occur in all phases and permits the design and development team to return to previous phases and review the findings and results of that stage (see Figure14-2). If necessary, the results of a previous stage can be altered.

The advantage of the iterative approach is that it tends to produce a better fit with user requirements, not only because it allows the results of previous phases to be corrected, but because it employs a much higher degree of user involvement than the waterfall approach. The iterative approach is characterised by a repeated loop in which

- the developers talk to the users and examine the business system and its information structures
- create a data design which they think may satisfy the user organisation's needs
- show this solution to the users, to verify that it is correct

The iterations do not go on for ever, of course. There has to be point at which the developers decide that the system is ready to be delivered to the users — normally after two or three iterations.

The main disadvantages of the iterative approach are that it

- uses more of the organisation's staff time
- is much more difficult to manage, because phases and tasks are not formally fixed

Data modelling is vitally important whichever approach or mixture of approaches is used, but is particularly suited to the iterative approach because

- graphical design methods allow users to see the design before it is implemented
- intensive user involvement allows the development of designs which are closer to the real information structures of the organisation
- good data modelling produces designs which are more easily changed without corrupting the integrity of the design

It is the contention of many practitioners in industry that if a thorough study of the user organisation is carried out and a good data model is derived based on the findings of the study of the organisation, then the resultant database will be able to fulfil all the processes and functions which the organisation could require. To design the data structures for a process, which is often the way it has been done in the past, only ensures that the data design will be able to support that process. It is fundamentally more sound to model the organisation's data structures rather than the data requirements of any particular process.

This underlines how important it is to derive a good working model of the organisation's information structures using both practical data modelling and a close involvement with the users within that organisation.

Feasibility

Data analysis skills are important even at the feasibility stage of a computer information systems project. One of the most important factors in determining the feasibility of a project and being able to estimate the level of difficulty that the designers will encounter in achieving the project's aims is to be able to assess the complexity of the information structures within the organisation. If the analyst is able to discuss the environment within which the system will operate, the analyst is able to assess whether the environment adheres to many of the standard models found in information systems.

The concepts of orders being placed by customers for products, for example, is a well-established paradigm in business information systems. The concepts of parts, assemblies and raw materials ordered from suppliers to be stored as stock before being used by assembly lines to make up products for customers are equally recognisable to an experienced systems analyst or data analyst. It is when the analyst encounters concepts which are difficult to grasp or requirements which appear to require very complex processing that the analyst will be able to recognise that a project may be more problematical than might have been first thought.

The involvement of competent systems analysts with good data modelling skills and knowledge are therefore important in the feasibility stage, if the feasibility report is to be an accurate view of the feasibility of the project.

Analysis and Design

The data analyst has always been central to the analysis phase of the project. It is at this point that the analyst learns as much as possible about all the organisation's functions and processes and the information structures that the organisation recognises. It is at this point that entities and their attributes are identified and the relationships between them determined.

The draft models in the form of ERMs are presented to the users who are then able to verify the analysts' understanding of the organisation. DFDs are employed to prove that processes can be supported by the data model. ELHs are employed to ensure that all events in the life of an entity have been considered and to detect other entities which may be implied as a result of the interaction between entities and the processes which cause the events in the entities' life. Normalisation is used to check that the data structures are properly designed, that all attributes are located with the correct entities, that there is no duplication, and that data is not stored in a way which makes it difficult to access.

The analysis phase is perhaps the point at which the data analyst's presence and input is most vital.

First Prototype

The first prototype is not a phase which is found in the classic waterfall approach to systems building. In the waterfall approach the users have little or no contact with the development team from the analysis phase to the point at which the finished system is installed in the user organisation, faults and all. In the iterative approach, the data design is quickly implemented as a database and shown to the users to elicit their responses both positive and negative. The database can be quickly populated with real data from the organisation's paper system, which makes it easier for the users to spot discrepancies between what they are used to and what the new system is displaying.

Those processes which may seem more complex than simple examination, manipulation and reporting of linked entities are also built and demonstrated. The demonstrations provide both user and developer the opportunity to better understand what is required of the system, what the proposed system is actually delivering and to make corrections to specifications, assumptions and design.

Iterative Development

After the first prototype of the database and the complex processes has been

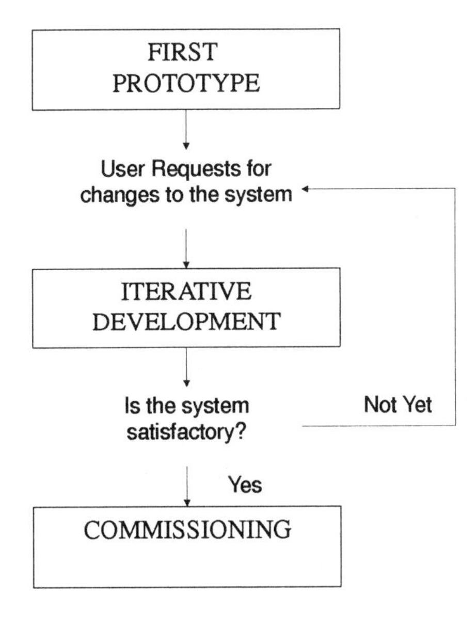

Figure 14-3 The Iterative Development Loop

The iterative process of demonstrate, consider and apply change requests, demonstrate occurs until the system is satisfactory. No more than three or four iterations should be necessary

demonstrated, the development team will make the necessary corrections and adjustments to the data design and the processes and will then return to the users for the second iteration (see Figure 14-3). All changes that were requested by the users following the demonstrations are carefully and formally noted. Not all changes will be implemented and all those that are implemented will be thoroughly documented.

Once again the users' responses, positive or negative are noted. This process of iteration continues, probably once or twice more until the developers feel that a point of diminishing returns has been reached. This often happens when a user, considering deeply some small detail, asks for it to be changed — back to the way it was in the first prototype. The iterative approach sometimes creates a culture of change for change's sake, and at this point the system is bolted down.

Commissioning

Commissioning, the most neglected of all phases of systems development, is one of the most important. The system must now be put in place in front of the users, not as a theoretical thing, but as an integrated part of the users' everyday work. The users must now be trained to use the system, must come to accept it as a useful aspect of their work and to develop a sense of ownership not only of the system's functions but of the data which resides within the system and upon which the system depends.

The involvement of the data analyst at this stage is helpful because of the thorough understanding of the business which the good analyst will have developed during previous phases. Furthermore, the analyst, because of very frequent contact with the users, should have developed an excellent working relationship with them, and will be able to assist in the process of integrating the new system into the business system.

It is a feature of the iterative approach to systems development that the twin elements of education in the use of the system and the adoption of ownership of it are achieved more quickly. This is because the users have been seeing the system grow and develop with their input. They are already familiar with it, have already established its importance to their jobs and already feel a sense of ownership due to being intimately involved in its creation.

System Evolution

Following the commissioning of the system, the data analyst remains involved with the project in order to ensure that subsequent changes to the system are carried out without damaging or degrading the design of the information structures. Whether maintenance is seen as a corrective process following system completion and delivery or whether it is seen as a naturally on-going process of enhancement, augmentation, growth and evolution, the data analyst must be involved to protect the integrity of the design. If the original design was thorough and complete, the data structures should be flexible enough to change with the changing needs of the organisation.

Those changes that are applied to the database design after delivery, however, must be applied with the same rigorous practices of good practical data modelling as the original development. The data analysts' involvement at this stage may be taken over by the Database Administrator, who should have as good data modelling skills and knowledge as the original data analysts. The role of the Database Administrator will be discussed in the next chapter.

Developing Database Applications

Summary

- The Waterfall Approach has a sequence of steps that, once completed, cannot be revisited
- The Iterative Approach assumes:

  that errors, omissions and misconceptions will occur

  that previous steps will be revisited and the results of previous steps corrected or improved

  that user involvement will be frequent and intensive in order to verify the ongoing design
- The Data Analyst, or other named developers possessing good practical data modelling skills, should be involved at all stages in the development life cycle

  In the *Feasibility Phase*, to use experience and skill in detecting complex data structures or processes which may make development difficult

  In the *Analysis and Design Phase*, to elicit an understanding of the user organisation's data structures and information needs, and to design the information structures to be implemented as a database

  In the *First Prototype Phase*, to be able to assess the impact of desired changes and discuss the advantages and disadvantages of changes with the users

  In the *Iterative Development Phase*, to flex and adjust the data structures in accordance with user change requests, while protecting the integrity of the design

  During the *Commissioning Phase* to employ a well-developed knowledge of the user organisation and familiarity with the users to assist the users in learning to use the system and to help them develop ownership

  In the *Evolutionary Development Phase* to make ongoing changes to the systems design in response to changing user needs

CHAPTER 15

INFORMATION RESOURCE MANAGEMENT

☐ **The Management of Information — Evolutionary Information Systems — The Corporate Information Edge — The Database Administrator (DBA) — Database Philosophy**

The Management of Information

In this chapter, we will be looking at those aspects of the data analyst's role which impact on the management of information as a resource and which continue after the initial analysis and design process is complete. Once the database has been designed and built, once the data is in place and the processes which act upon this data are operating smoothly, the data analyst becomes involved in the evolution of the database and the system which makes use of it. Now the analyst is responsible for *maintaining* and *managing* the database definition. Aspects of the data analysts's tasks also relate to the security and the integrity of the information held in the database.

Evolutionary Information Systems

For a long time, there has been an understanding among those people who design and build computer systems — that once the process of designing and building is complete, the job is over. Whilst such an attitude may have been appropriate in years gone by it is rapidly becoming outdated.

More and more people are talking about evolutionary information systems: systems which develop in an evolutionary way using prototyping and very fast and flexible ways of building and changing systems.

The data analyst is involved in this process of evolution in much the same way as during the design — as a person who analyses the needs of the organisation and analyses the structures of the organisation's information. However, instead of creating the database definition, the analyst is now maintaining the definition of the database.

Database

A database is an integrated and planned structure of related information about a real world information environment. A database can be seen as a model of the real world, keeping itself, via its processes, as close as possible to a one-to-one relationship with the real world which it is modelling. The relationship between the real world and the representation of the real world held as data in the database is highly important, because the closer a database reflects the real world, the more appropriate will be the decisions and actions taken by the organisation on the basis of the information in the system.

Conversely, a system which reflects its real-world environment poorly may well lead to serious errors in decision making and to inappropriate actions being taken.

A database which does not change once it is set up will very quickly become out of date, and will, depending on the degree of change in the real world, soon become so unworkable that it will have to be abandoned. The more modern approaches to analysis and design attempt to alleviate the problem of degradation of design by building the system in a flexible way. If the system is designed for change, in order to allow a prototyping approach, it will continue to be able to change after delivery.

The modern world of computer systems cannot any longer afford to accept the doctrine of build, maintain and scrap when it comes to computer systems. Enormous resources are required to redesign, re-code, and reimplement a system when a quantum jump is required to keep up with changes in the organisational environment. As systems get bigger and more complex, holding more and more information, the problem will get worse. Furthermore, the pace of change in the systems environment (the real world in which systems operate) is getting faster and faster. It is also an unfortunate fact that the vast majority of programmers and analysts are engaged in maintaining inflexible and badly designed systems, rather than creating new systems or significantly enhancing existing systems. This maintenance can be made very problematical by designs which were never meant to be changed.

Systems are usually composed of subsystems, and it is the scrapping and redesign and rebuild of the subsystems which produces the alternate periods of stability and of sudden change in traditional systems (see Figure 15-1).

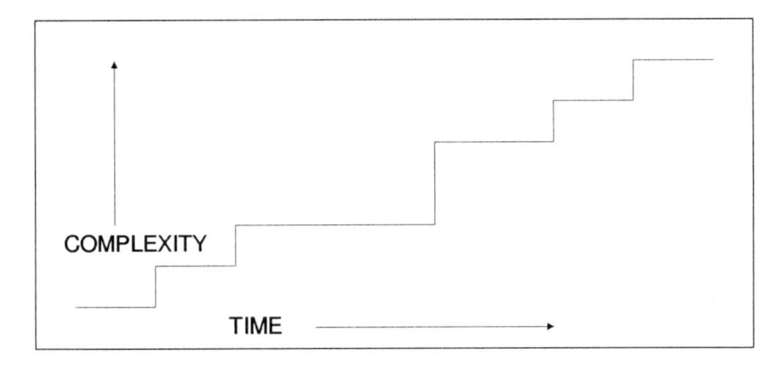

Figure 15-1 The Discrete System Stepped Line

The system changes in large jumps when subsystems become unworkable and are scrapped, rewritten and recoded.

Maintenance must be seen as grouped into a number of very different exercises:

- fixing bugs, programming faults or errors which should never have been in the system in the first place and which were *not* in the specification
- changing the design or programming of the existing system so that it actually does what the users needed in the first place, even though the existing system *does* adhere to the specification
- adding a new feature or facility which the user organisation now needs because the environment within which it operates has changed

All these types of maintenance are made far more difficult if the system is not designed to be flexible, especially if the underlying data structures in the database have not been designed using good data modelling practices.

This suggests that it is becoming preferable for systems to be inherently flexible and to evolve in small steps rather than in large leaps. Instead of a system being built and put in place over a number of years and then being discarded when the poorly designed core and the layers of corrective maintenance become unworkable, the system should be built to accommodate change and should change smoothly in response to changing business needs (see Figure 15-2).

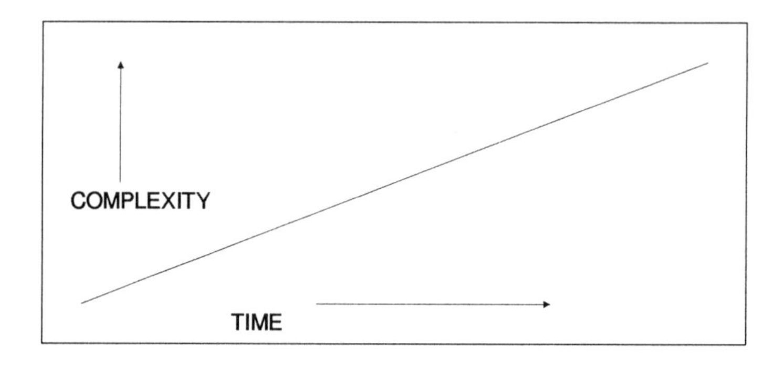

Figure 15-2 The Smooth Evolutionary Curve

With good underlying design, the system should be able to adapt to the changes in the organisation's needs in small, as-needed increments.

Fourth Generation Development

It would be sad, in a book on practical data modelling, and especially in a chapter on information resource management and evolutionary information systems, not to mention the emergent Fourth Generation approach to systems building. The use of the term Fourth Generation Language (4GL) is deceptive and has only arisen out of historical accident. A far better term is a 4GE or *Fourth Generation Environment.*

A 4GE is a software tool or set of tools which allow the fast development of information systems. A 4GE operates within a narrow domain of applications and has an underlying engine which tends to determine the style of the system being produced. It is usually composed of:

- a database (including a powerful dictionary facility)
- a data definition language (DDL)
- a data manipulation language (DML)
- a powerful report generator
- a screen and menu generator
- a graphical output generator

These tools, used in conjunction with prototyping, will often produce a system which is more in tune with user expectations and needs, and which, due to the inherent flexibility of the approach, will be more flexible following delivery to the user. The evolutionary approach to building systems has its drawbacks. It tends to be a more expensive and time consuming approach involving far more of user's time than more traditional approaches. However, the extra time and resources required are normally regained by lower maintenance costs. It is also particularly suited to systems development projects which are:

- primarily to do with business or organisational information handling systems
- systems which are less well defined than average
- systems which change dynamically at a faster rate than average

4GEs have one more characteristic — they require very good data modelling skills. The length of time taken to develop a system in a 4GE may be remarkably short in comparison with the timescales involved in more traditional methods of development. However, if the tools are misused or if good data modelling is not carried out, they can produce systems which are very poor and require as much (if not more) maintenance as traditional approaches.

Data Modelling

Data modelling, then, will become accepted, if it is not already, as a discipline of not just creating databases, not just maintaining them, but of allowing them to grow and flex smoothly in response to the business or organisation's changes.

More and more organisations are realising that to maintain a competitive edge in the market-place, they must rely more and more on information systems. This applies whether or not the organisation is profit making.

Many organisations today are struggling to deal with a legacy of poor design of databases. These databases were not built using good data modelling and are not properly normalised. Because of this there are often problems of data duplication and poor access between files which should be keyed together but which are not. Very little data at the present time is stored in well-designed databases run by good database management systems (DBMS).

It is of tremendous value to the organisation to have all information accurate, up-to-date and accessible instantly in a wide variety of forms of presentation. To achieve this end, the organisation concerned must adopt a policy of database philosophy.

Database Philosophy

Database philosophy is a corporate policy of adhering to proper database practices. These include;

- designing for strategic objectives
- data stored once only
- data stored in a single database
- designing for fast, flexible access
- designing to reduce wasted database space
- central control of database changes
- all data security under management control

These practices lead to a number of benefits:

- greater accuracy and reliability of information
- information is available more quickly
- better security and protection of data
- easier and more flexible access to information
- computer equipment holds more data and performs better

- systems are more likely to serve corporate plans
- systems will adapt more easily to changing corporate needs

These benefits can only be achieved by putting in place a database philosophy policy. There is no other way.

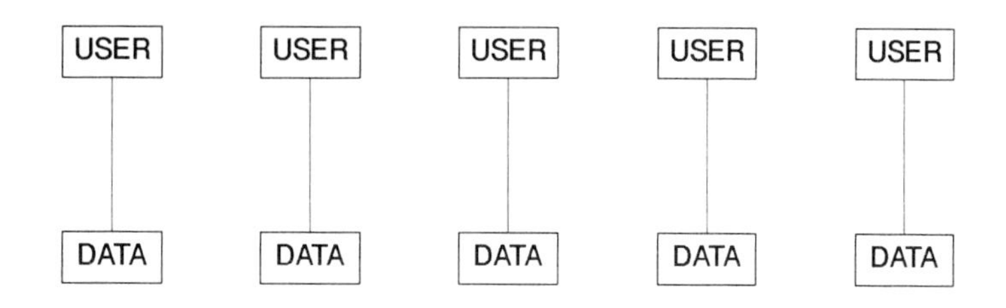

Figure 15-3 Disconnected Data Structures

All users have their own store of data. Data cannot be shared, strategic planning of data storage is extremely difficult , duplication of information is likely, access security is absent and data integrity control is normally poor.

Disconnected Data Structures

Many businesses are struggling with disconnected data structures (see Figure 15-3). In environments where the data structures are disconnected, a number of problems occur.

- Local ownership of data does not serve the organisation

  When access to the corporate database is not easy, or when users find that they do not trust data held by someone else, little databases spring up within a company to fulfil the needs of local users. Because the users own this data and use it, and have problems if it is bad data, they will often maintain the data in this database with great care. However, someone in the organisation outside this local group may well require access to the data

- Disconnected sets of data held separately may need to be linked for some reason

  It may be that management has a requirement to compare the profile of customers stored in the customer invoicing database by the accounting division with the profiles of prospects stored by the marketing division. Even obtaining a single list of customers may be a problem, if each regional sales office maintains its own PC-based database

- The capability of the local databases to respond to corporate environmental changes is minimal

It is relatively easy for a computer literate user to set up a simple, un-normalised data table in a PC database such as dBase or PowerHouse. This data table may be all the users need and may work perfectly well. But the computer literate user who set up the database is probably much less capable of judging when and how it needs to be changed when it starts to fail to fulfil the local group's needs. As to how to go about changing the data structures, porting or updating the new database from the old, setting up a classification data table to improve code validation — forget it. Only a professional can carry out such functions effectively.

For these reasons, an integrated database, well-organised and controlled, is the only really effective way of properly utilising and managing an organisation's information (See Figure 15-4).

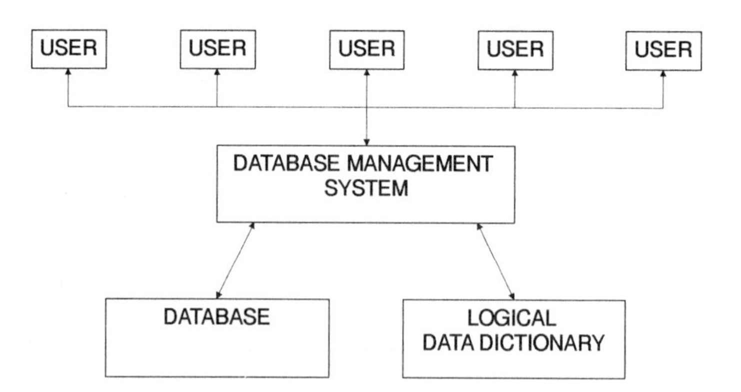

Figure 15-4 Integrated Data Structure

All users and applications access the same database, via a Database Management System which controls access security and manages the physical database.

The Database Administrator

When the data modelling has been done, and the database which the organisation needs has been built, it is not the end of the story. When, for example, a car is designed and built by an automotive manufacturer, after its sale to a customer, it has to have regular maintenance, it has to be kept locked up when not in use (hopefully in a garage), it may possibly benefit from some enhancements and after some time has passed it will have to have repairs and may need worn parts replacing. Once a database has been created and is in regular use, exactly the same things need to be dealt with. The database needs to be managed and protected effectively.

The Database Administrator (DBA) is the person in an organisation who is responsible for the supervision and control of the database (see Figure15-5).

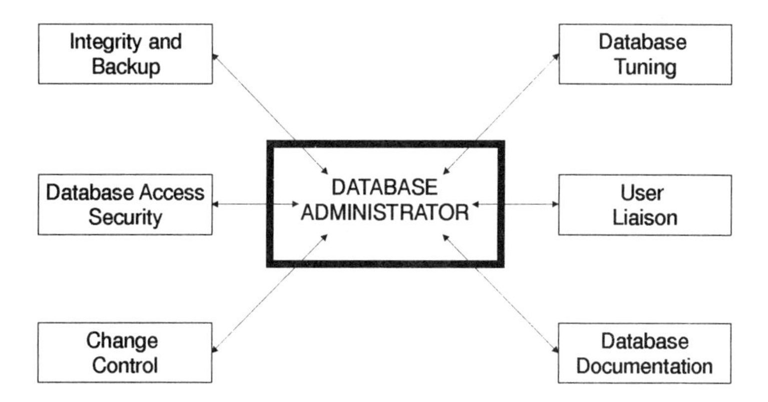

Figure 15-5 The Database Administrator's Tasks

The DBA is a vital member of the systems team, with far-reaching responsibility for the security, integrity and accessibility of the organisation's information.

A good development team leader will ensure that a DBA is appointed from among the design team, and given responsibility for the management of the database and the dictionary even during the development period. Such a job can only be carried out by an experienced and skilled data analyst who has a thorough training in practical data modelling.This job, once the development team has handed over the systems to the users and to the team which will maintain it, is often transferred to the DBA appointed by the user organisation.

Very few organisations have a dedicated DBA on the payroll, but, inevitably, most organisations which have a database have some person who — at least in theory — have the Database Administrator's tasks as their responsibility. It is a sad fact that most organisations possessing a database are very lax about looking after it post implementation. Very few of the formal tasks of the DBA are carried out effectively. These tasks are:

- database access security
- integrity and backup
- change control
- database tuning
- user liaison
- database documentation

Database Access Security

As has already been mentioned, the data that is held in the database of any organisation which uses its information systems as an integral part of its activities is very valuable. The loss of the data will result in the high costs of reconstruction and at worst the complete failure of the organisation. It is therefore vital that the data is protected. Most modern database management systems have inbuilt facilities for controlling access to the data. These will often allow the users to be individually identified by a usercode and allowed access to the database only by a password.

Users may also be classified into groups, which makes the sensitive restriction of access easier for the DBA. Users are then given such access to the database as is necessary for them to do their job effectively. Staff working in the technical department may not need to see or update the customer files, for example, and staff who do need access to the customer files will probably not need access to the files of parts or work in progress in the factory. This is all dependent on the kind of job that the person does and what tasks they carry out in the course of their duties.

For example, the following SQL statements carry out a number of security functions within the database management system. Specific levels of access to the database system have been either *grant*ed or *revoke*d to or from specific users, with the password specified in the case of *grant*.

```
grant connect to JSMITH identified by FHHTYBBB;

grant dba to SYSMANAGER5 identified by OMKJOKUR;

revoke dba from JBROWN;
```

Database Administrator 'power' has been *grant*ed to the user identified by SYSMANAGER5. This level of power is *grant*ed very rarely because it gives the user the power to *grant* access to the system for new users or *revoke* access from existing users.

In the following statement, the privilege to add or change a record in the CUSTOMERS table has been given to two users. These users, of course, will have previously been *grant*ed access to the database system.

```
grant insert, update on CUSTOMERS to JSMITH, PJONES;
```

It may also be possible, in some database management systems, to attach security classifications to datasets (files or entity stores), to individual records (rows in the table) or to individual attributes (columns in the table). It may be possible to group these under a single logical name to allow security rules to be set up more easily.

Once these classifications have been set up, users or groups of users may be allowed or denied access to any item or items of data. Accesses take many forms, all of which are very different in their level of power and the damage they can do. The accepted set of standard access forms (sometimes called permissions or capabilities) is:

- Read

  The user or users have the power to look at the data only. All other forms of access are prevented. This is also called enquiry, read only or view.

  It may be desirable, for example, to restrict an enquiry clerical officer to only be able to read the one file that they are responsible for in answering customer telephone queries.

- Add

  The user or user group are able to add new records to the dataset.

  A common form of fraud is the improper creation of suppliers and invoices payable, which allows forged payable invoices to be set up. Cheques are then raised automatically — and may not be scrutinised very carefully in a large company — and sent to the defrauder's home address. Add capability is only applicable to staff with supervisory roles and must be carefully controlled.

- Delete

  The user or group may delete items of data from the record, may delete the record altogether or may be able to delete the entire dataset, depending on what data the delete capability is allowed for.

  Careless allocation of delete can be disastrous. Most people who have experience with computer systems are aware of the devastating results of one of the many 'delete all' commands. Recovery will be complex, dangerous and expensive, if it is possible at all. Delete capability is also a possible route for fraud.

- Change

  The user or group of users may make changes to data which already exists in the data records. This is also called update, modify or alter.

  Change capability is also very open to fraud. For example, if the internal file of cheque data ready to be printed is not adequately protected, the name and address of the payee could be changed by a member of staff — to their own name and home address. If not protected, an amount of £10.00 could be changed to any amount.

The accesses *add*, *change* and *delete* are collectively referred to as write or update because all of them involve making modifications to the data.

The control of these forms of access by users is central to the security of the database and the data it contains. The Database Administrator must be aware of the security facilities in the database, the needs and dangers of user access and the nature of the data and its sensitivity.

Clearly, different environments will have different data security needs. What is more, the tighter the security the more restrictive the users will find the system, thus defeating its purpose, which is to supply information. The more sensitive and detailed the security, the more costly the task of controlling security on a day-to-day basis. The DBA must balance all the needs, dangers and the available budget and provide the system with the best security.

Views

A view is a logical window on the database, that does not actually exist in its own right as a dataset, but is a defined way of looking at an existing dataset or datasets. Views are particularly useful for sensitive security control. If, for example, the database designer or DBA wished to allow access to read a customer file, but did not wish to allow users to see the year-to-date sales for that company, a view could be created which contained all the customer data except the data item *sales-year-to-date*.

Users could then be given free access to the created customer file view, without compromising the sensitive data. It is jointly the responsibility of the data analyst and the DBA to establish which views may be needed by the users. Views are a special kind of dataset — one that does not physically exist in its own right in the database. Once the actual data sets have been created, it is possible in several database management systems to create a view. The view contains no data of its own, but is simply a redefinition of other datasets. Any changes to the real data stores will cause the data seen by looking at the view to change.

For example, the customer file and the invoice file may be set up as stores of data. A view may then be created which appears to contain some (not all) elements of the customer file and some elements of the invoice file, linked together so that the view contains the invoices for the customer that has been accessed.

The following code demonstrates how SQL can be used to create a view.

```
create view
        car_service as
        select registration_number, make, type of service
        from car, service
        where car.registration_number =
```

```
service.registration_number;
```

The view created is called *car_service*, and will retrieve only the specified data items from the tables *car* and *service*, joined by the key *registration_number*.

Metadata Security

The data in the database has to be protected, but the metadata, too, needs to be controlled. The actual definition of the data structures within the database is a very sensitive issue. Only the DBA or an authorised data analyst should have access to the metadata for update. The contents of the data dictionary are the very skeleton and foundation of the database and if the metadata were changed by an unauthorised person, the database's operation could be seriously impaired.

The definition of attribute and entity names, the labels used for reporting or in on-screen interfaces, the indices which link the files together and the security definitions in the database are clearly highly sensitive and only a very few carefully vetted and qualified individuals should be allowed access to these definitions.

Integrity and Backup

The data stored in the database represents an enormous investment in time and expense. Its loss will lead to much expense and trouble at the least — at worst, the failure of the company. Backup and integrity are therefore paramount.

The DBA, having an understanding of the database, its various datasets and their relationships, must be involved in the planning of backup. It is simply not sufficient to backup the whole system on a regular basis. Many database management systems provide a facility to backup all or part of the database quite separately from the rest of the system.

The DBA might decide, for example that a certain dataset, such as one which holds transactions which are added at the rate of thousands per hour, must be backed up every 30 minutes. This would mean that a serious system failure would mean the loss of only up to 30 minutes transactions, instead of the tens of thousands of transactions which might be lost — those since the last daily backup. The design of an effective and sensitive backup schedule is an essential aspect of the DBA's role.

Change Control Document		
System	Program Reference	
Requested By	Department	Date
Details of Change Required		
Change Justification		
Impact Estimate (*Programs/Database Definition*)		
Resource Estimate		
Approved By	Authority	Date
Design Impact	Entered To LDD By	Date
Assigned For Maintenance To		Date
Change Completed (Initials)		Date
Maintenance Documentation Completed		Date

Figure 15-6 An Example Change Control Document

The Change Control Document is a vital element in managing change in the system and the underlying database design.

Change Control

In many environments, change control is carried out informally, but in environments which are managed professionally, all change requests are recorded on a change control document by the analysis team and are carefully vetted (see Figure 15-6). Change control is often neglected in systems environments. Changes requested by users are implemented without consideration of the cost-benefit of the change and without adequate assessment of impact on other aspects of the system or on the system documentation.

Change requests which require changes to the database structure as defined in the data dictionary must be carefully vetted by the DBA. Only the DBA or an equivalent person with extensive responsibility for and knowledge of the database design can make reasoned decisions as to what should be changed, how it should be changed and when it should be changed. In a large organisation, the database and the DBA may serve tens of thousands of users and groups of users, all of varying levels of seniority and strategic knowledge and with widely differing tactical objectives. The needs of users, when they conflict, must be resolved, if necessary at a higher level of authority. Otherwise, the data analyst, in conjunction with a senior user, must make a choice between them.

Database Tuning

The database structures as implemented in the disk drives or other storage devices, either automatically by the database management system or with some human input, have considerable implications for access speed and other performance factors. There are considerations which are solely to do with the hardware and operating systems software, such as the percentage of free record space in a dataset which uses a system calculated key for direct access.

However, other considerations for performance depend entirely on the design of the database, and in such cases, the DBA's involvement is essential. Even the design of programs for performance may require a detailed understanding of the database structures and should involve the DBA's expertise.

For example, a dataset in the database may be changed in order to allow fast keying directly to a field or attribute which was not previously keyed. This may mean that programs which accessed this dataset may work far more efficiently if the change to the data design is carried through into the program design. The DBA, as guardian of the database design, should be involved in the redesign of such programs.

User Liaison

The DBA should be a senior member of staff. Only by giving the DBA a level of seniority equal to the responsibility of the job and the impact of information resource management on the organisation can the DBA attract sufficient respect from users and software developers to carry out their duties properly. There will be a number of political pressures placed on the DBA from senior management, who after all, have the job of maximising the resources available to their own spheres of operation. The DBA must have the seniority to be able to balance these pressures impartially. An important aspect of the DBA's duties is liaising with users, at every level of the organisation.

Pressure for changes to the systems will be directed in the first instance at development teams responsible for particular areas of the business software. In strategic situations, however, where a major conceptual change is required to the database structures, the impact of change will be widespread and the DBA should be involved in discussions with both users and the development teams to decide on the strategic changes to be made.

The DBA therefore must be a member of staff who is able to communicate effectively with both users and with development staff. In this respect the DBA must be a hybrid, skilled and experienced in both the technical aspects of systems and database design and in the objectives and working practices of the business organisation.

Database Documentation

Many database management systems may contain an inherent built-in documentation facility. the names of entities (implemented as datasets) and attributes (implemented as fields in the datasets) will certainly be internally documented in the metadata. More sophisticated DBMSs may well have facilities for textual descriptions or explanations to be stored with more basic database definition metadata. Other information, such as validation tests, triggers which control the integrity of data, internally stored definitions of screens and reports or other programs may also be stored within the database management system itself.

More commonly, the DBMS only allows storage of the most basic information about the database. Information about changes, resulting from the well-considered change control mechanisms discussed earlier, will probably have to be stored separately from the database.

In either case, whether metadata is stored automatically internally by the DBMS or whether metadata has to be stored separately, it is the DBA who has (or should have) ultimate responsibility for ensuring that the documentation of the database is complete, up-to-date and accurate.

The Data Analyst and Data Security

The data analyst, during the analysis phase in which documents and users are interrogated to determine the database design, will encounter a tremendous amount of information about what is to be stored and why, who needs access to it, and what kinds of access are needed. During the process of data analysis and design, then, is an ideal time to begin compiling the security details of the database. As has already been discussed, many data dictionaries or DBMSs have the facilities for defining and enforcing the data security rules as well as other aspects of the system metadata.

All the security tasks and functions carried out by the DBA which have just been discussed are therefore based on the security information which is defined during the analysis phase by the analyst. Data analysis and design is then not just to do with creating a data model, but about protecting that data model and the information which will reside within it. Security is often neglected as part of the data analyst's job, and questions have been raised as to whether the security of the database has anything to do with the data analyst in the first place. Who is better placed to be able to identify

- all data files and their fields
- all pertinent users
- all the forms of access needed to files by users?

A good data analyst will consider aspects of security within the model when designing the model for implementation as a database.

Database Management Systems (DBMS)

A relational database management system (RDBMS) will normally have all the facilities necessary to achieve the objectives of a database philosophy. Simply buying an RDBMS will not achieve them.

The RDBMS must be used intelligently and in a well-planned way. The best RDBMS in the world cannot design your database structures for you — that is what data modelling is all about. The most elegant security facilities will not protect the database unless it is used intelligently. This means training information systems staff, training users, putting in place a competent DBA and adopting practices throughout the systems development area — indeed, the whole company — which fit in with the IRM strategy.

Information Resource Management

Summary

- The size, complexity and rate of change of modern information systems using complex databases suggest that an evolutionary approach (change by small increments), rather than scrap and rebuild, may be an effective strategy
- Fourth generation environments (4GE) are software tools allowing fast build of business information systems (and subsequent evolutionary change) and include:

  database
  data dictionary
  data definition language (DDL)
  data manipulation language (DML)
  screen and menu generator
  report generator or data query language (DQL)

- 4GEs require good data modelling skills because the software engines driving the 4GE tools require a well-considered relational model
- Database philosophy is a strategic management policy of gathering, controlling and managing information, involving

  designing for strategic objectives
  data stored once only
  data stored in a single database
  design for fast, flexible database access
  designing to reduce wasted database space
  central control of database changes

- The effective Database Administrator will certainly have data analysis skills (including practical data modelling) as well as management skills
- The Database Administrator's tasks include

  database access security
  integrity and backup
  change control

database tuning

user liaison

database documentation

- The data analyst should take advantage of the data analysis and design phase to identify security details, including

  who needs access to what information in the database

  what form of access are required (read only, change, delete, add)

  what datasets (implemented from entities) and what fields (attributes) will be accessed by whom and in what way

FURTHER READING

Those who find the subject of data modelling needs further exploration may find the following list helpful.

- Ashworth, C. and Goodland, M., *SSADM: A Practical Approach*, McGraw-Hill, 1990

  A thorough, start-to-finish guide to SSADM, in all its detail.

- Brooks, F.P., *The Mythical Man-Month*, Addison-Wesley, 1982

  A very readable and philosophical series of essays on the development of software systems, including the need to design for inevitable change and debunking the idea that twice as many people will do the job twice as fast.

- Chen, P.P., *The Entity Relationship Model — Towards a Unified View of Data,* Association for Computing Machinery Transactions on Database Systems, Volume 1, Number 1

  This is the original refereed paper which first established the concepts of entity relationship modelling. It appeared in the first issue of the journal American Computing Machinery Transactions on Database Systems and any data analyst who wishes to hold their own in conversation concerning data design theory should have read it. It is remarkably obtuse but very seminal.

- Date, C.J., *An Introduction to Database Systems Volume I* (5th Edition), Addison-Wesley, 1990

  This sizable book has an enormous coverage and is a must for anyone to wants to obtain a thorough understanding of most aspects of the subject of databases. The author is very highly respected in the field.

- DeMarco, T., *Structured Analysis and System Specification*, Yourdon Press, 1978

  This is an excellent book, mainly concerned with the development cycle and with the analysis and specification of processes. The conventions for Data Flow Diagrams in this book have been taken from DeMarco.

- Harry, M., *Information and Management Systems*, Pitman, 1990

  An examination of systems (not just computer systems) and how they develop and are controlled. A good coverage of approaches to creating information systems, including how to approach the building of systems which are less than clear in their requirements.

- Howe D.R., *Data Analysis for Database Design*, Edward Arnold, 1989

  A very thorough and detailed coverage of E-R modelling, with only brief coverage of normalisation. This is a text for students and contains exercises and answers.

- Liebenau, J. and Backhouse, J., *Understanding Information: An Introduction*, MacMillan, 1990

  A very readable examination of information as a subject in its own right. Deals in a straightforward (and in places new) way with semiology, the study of the relationship between information and the real world represented by the information.

- Smith, A.N. and Medley, D.B., *Information Resource Management*, South-Western Publishing, 1987

  Covers the organisational and management perspective of information resource management from planning and controlling development of systems, through security and integrity of the information, to dealing with people. An excellent non-technical work oriented towards professionals and management.

GLOSSARY OF TERMS

Using the glossary

This glossary is provided both as a means of summarising explanations in the main text and as a quick-reference guide to the terminology of ER modelling. Other terms relevant to database design and database systems development have been included.

Most of the terms in this glossary may be found in the main index, where references to other pages may be found.

- 3NF

  See Third Normal Form

- 4GE

  See Fourth Generation Environment

- Attribute

  An item of information about an entity, information owned by an entity. Equivalent to a column in a table, or a field in a record.

- Database

  A structured collection of related information. Often computerised, within a Database Management System (DBMS).

- Database Administrator

  Officer of an organisation responsible for the proper maintenance of the database, including ongoing data modelling and design, tuning, user security, access security and physical design.

- Database Philosophy

  The management philosophy of once-only storage of data, involving database policy, management information and decision support services and the proper protection, control and use of information.

- Data Flow Diagram

  A simple graphical representation of an information handling process or processes, used by the data analyst to analyse, verify and confirm information flows.

- DBA

  See Database Administrator

- DBMS

  See Relational Database Management System

- Default Membership

  Type C of Howe's four types, where the one end of a one-to-many relationship has optional membership (the relationship with the *many* end may or may not exist) and the *many* end has mandatory membership (the relationship to the one end must exist).

- Degree of Relationship

  One of one-to-one, one-to-many and many-to-many, the three possible types of relationship on the ERM.

- Denormalisation

  The practice of changing tables which are in Third Normal Form so that they break one or more rules of normalisation. Normally done for performance reasons.

- DFD

  See Data Flow Diagram

- ELH

  See Entity Life History

- Entity

  A thing which is uniquely identifiable, the owner of attributes or characteristics and which is of interest to the organisation. People, events, places, documents and abstract concepts and objects may all be entities. Some entities exist only for the purpose of the operation of the data model.

- Entity, Link

  A weak entity which exists to decompose a many-to-many relationship.

- Entity, Lookup

  A weak entity, normally an attribute, stored separately to reduce duplication, improve input validation and allowing flexible classification of the entity.

- Entity, Strong

  An object, person or event about which information is to be stored. The entity must be uniquely identifiable, must be the owner of information (attributes).

- Entity, Weak

  An entity which exists functionally only with reference to strong entities. E.g. an *order-line* entity cannot exist without the *order* entity. See also Entity, Link.

- Entity Life History

  A simple diagrammatic representation of the various processes or information flows which impact on an entity, including changes in status of the entity. Describes all states or processes through which an entity may pass, including its birth and death events.

- Entity Relationship Model

  A simple diagrammatic representation of the information structure of an organisation, showing all the entities (information objects) and their relationships. It is used by the data analyst to analyse, record and confirm aspects of the data model.

- ERM

  See Entity Relationship Model

- Foreign Key

  The unique identifier of one table inserted into another table, thus implementing the relationship between the two entities represented by the tables.

- Fourth Generation Environment

  A set of software tools which allow very fast development of flexible business systems. Composed of a DBMS, Dictionary, and software to generate screens, menus, reports and programs. May also include facilities for graphical output of information.

- Hybrid

  A person who possesses training and experience in both business and management, and in computing and IT, allowing the person to bridge any communication gap between users and information systems professionals.

- Information

  Any message, signal or facts received which are informative to the receiver. Data forms the raw material for information, but must be converted into a state which is accurate, timely and meaningful in order to be information.

- Key

  Data item or items which can be used to directly access a particular record.

- LDD

  See Logical Data Dictionary

- Logical Data Dictionary (LDD)

  The repository of the metadata of an information system. The LDD may be compiled, textual or interactive. The LDD defines all the entities (in the form of tables), all the attributes (as columns of the tables) and relationships (as foreign keys in the tables). More sophisticated LDDs may also define details of validation, rules of access, security details and processes.

- Membership

  Whether an occurrence of an entity must or may take part in the relationship with another entity. When an entity must relate to another entity,the relationship is mandatory (also referred to as obligatory), when it may exist without a relationship with another entity the relationship is optional (also referred to as non-obligatory).

- Metadata

  Data about data. Data is the actual contents of the database as stored and accessed by users. Metadata defines the structure and form adopted by the data. Metadata may also include formatting, display and validation standards.

- Normalisation

  A technique of data analysis in which all data items are considered and their dependencies used to build tables for uniquely keyed items. Normalisation is slow and cumbersome and is often omitted in favour of Entity Relationship Modelling. The resultant tables are usually checked to ensure that they are well-normalised.

- Positional Semantics

  The use of position within the ERM to indicate the hierarchical structure of the data, enforced by the use of downward pointing tridents only.

- Relationship

  The existence of a link between two entities, whereby one entity may be owned by or associated with another.

- Relational Database Management System

  Software which is designed to control and manage a database, using relational structures (tables linked by indexed columns). Uses a data repository or dictionary to store the structure and definitions of the data. Sophisticated RDBMSs will also control the relationships between tables.

- Scope Diagram
- A zero-level Data Flow Diagram — which contains only one process (the system itself) and shows all flows of data to and from the system.
- Unnormalised Data

  Data which has not yet been examined by a data analyst and which may not adhere to Third Normal Form.
- User

  A person, or group of persons who access, read, add to, delete from, modify or use an information system. Normally distinct from the systems personnel, and often referring to non-technical business or organisational staff. Also referred to as *end-user.*
- Well-Normalised

  The condition of a table as obeying the rules for Normal forms, i.e. having no repeating groups, having no part-key dependencies and having no inter-data dependencies.
- Zero-Level DFD

  See Scope Diagram

APPENDIX A

SSADM

☐ **Elements — Phases — Place of Data Modelling — SSADM is a comprehensive methodology —Membership marking and normalisation in SSADM**

What Is SSADM?

SSADM is an abbreviation of *Structured Systems Analysis and Design Methodology*. SSADM is a formal methodology which attempts to address all aspects of the systems development life cycle (including detailed data analysis and design).

In 1981 SSADM was selected as the standard which had to be used for all UK government systems projects. SSADM follows the data-driven approach to systems design, that is, it assumes that there is a fundamental underlying data structure which will change little over the lifetime of a system. This is the philosophy put over in the main text of this book.

The techniques of Entity Relationship Modelling, Data Flow Diagramming, the diagramming of Entity Life Histories and the use of normalisation, all described in the main text of this book, were all adopted by and are all present in SSADM. As with most standards, SSADM reflects a well-established and therefore not state-of-the-art approach. Its approach as a methodology is very much in line with the waterfall way of thinking, and until recently had no elements of prototyping at all. The great benefits of SSADM lie not only in

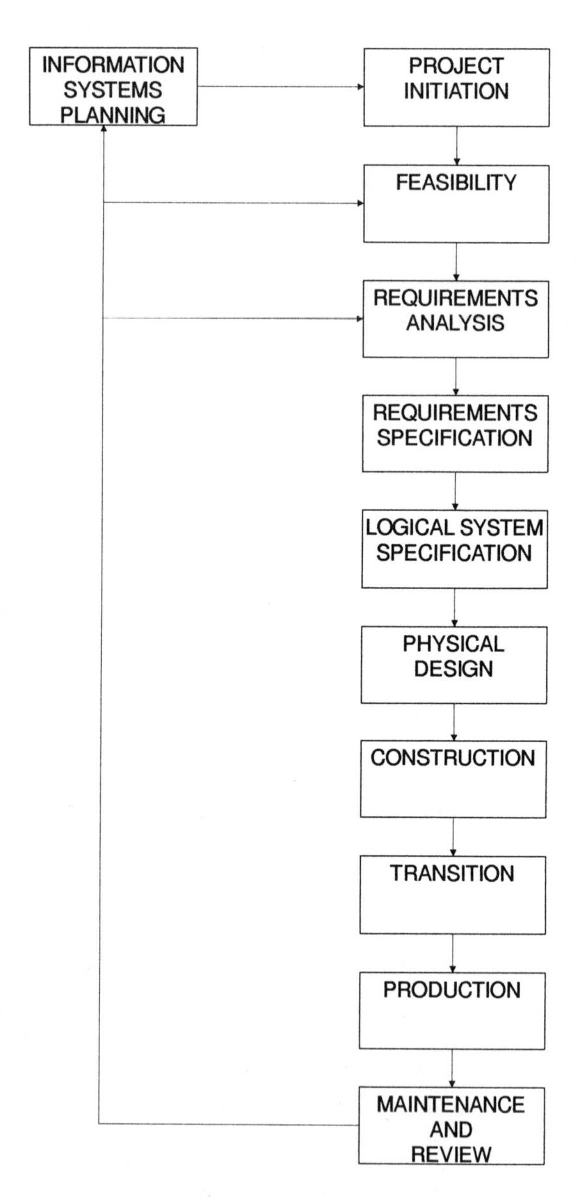

Figure A-1 The SSDAM System Development Life Cycle

its adoption of well-tried and standardised approaches and techniques, but in the way that it forces a formal, structured approach.

The use of the entity grid where every entity is charted against every other entity to detect all relationships, for example, is simply a way of forcing analysts to look at every aspect of the system. This is laudable in safety critical systems, for example, but it is often the case that analysts know from their understanding of the system under study that certain possibilities are not worth looking at. This might be called intuition, it might be called experience, but in many cases, some of the steps or methods forced upon analysts by SSADM (or any other rigid methodology for that matter) would appear irksome and unnecessary and would in all probability be circumvented to save wasting valuable time.

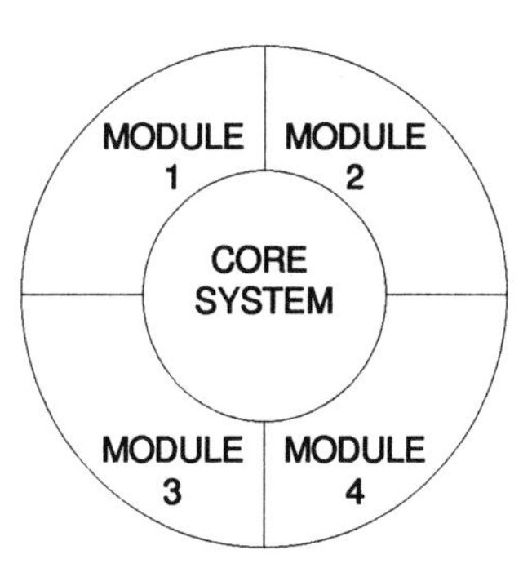

Figure A-2 Modules Implemented Around Core

Although SSADM does not advocate such an approach, the problems associated with a large project and a large development team can be reduced by implementing a core system, and adding modules .

The approach put forward in the main text of this book, while equally suitable for large-scale projects using the waterfall approach, strongly advocates modular and evolutionary ways of working (see Figure A-2). SSADM does not. It suggests an approach which carries out all analysis, followed by all design, followed by wholesale implementation of all aspects of the requirements. In such an approach, it is far more important to be painstaking in examining every small detail, in checking every assumption and conclusion numerous times and using multiple cross-checking techniques.

If a more evolutionary approach is used which allows for confirmation of design by the users *prior to delivery*, many of the details of SSADM become less essential and the time-intensive aspects of some of its detail may begin to outweigh some of its undoubted advantages.

Very few organisations use all of SSADM or follow it to the letter. It is an exhaustive system, with a great deal of detail. Most users of SSADM take only those of the techniques described by the methodology as are relevant or useful to the particular project.

Although SSADM has many faults, including a failure to address major sections of the system development life cycle and a tendency to be unwieldy, it has one very major advantage: that it is rapidly becoming a standard. This means that those techniques covered by SSADM have been given a standard way of doing the task.

Most people would agree that the techniques, steps and methods of SSADM are not to be followed religiously, except inasmuch as the user organisation requires it. It is certain that a project which uses SSADM will require a large team to utilise SSADM, whether or not a large team is required to deal with the project as a whole.

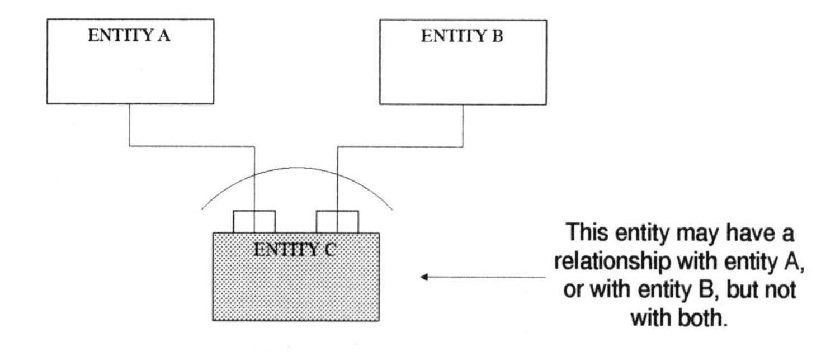

Figure A-3 Marking Exclusive Relationships

Exclusive Relationships In SSADM

Exclusive relationships are relationships which cannot occur together. In Figure A-3 , the arc drawn across the two relationship line indicates that the entity C at the many end may have a relationship with *either* entity A *or* entity

B but not both. This technique is a useful device, and is easily adopted for use in ER modelling. It requires special processing, of course, to implement this requirement in a relational database, and as such the data analyst may wish to limit or avoid its use.

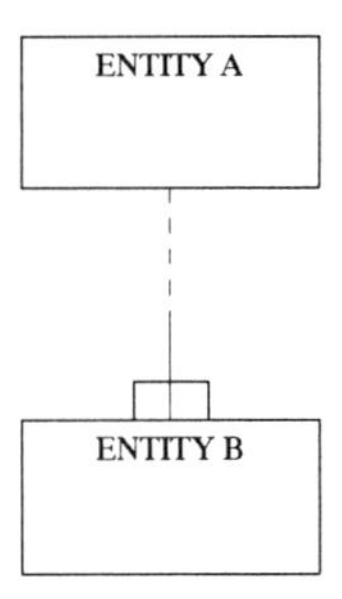

Figure A-4 Membership Marking in SSADM

Membership Marking In SSADM

In version 4, SSADM uses broken lines (see Figure A-4) to represent optionality. In this diagram entity A does not have to take part in the relationship. The one end is optional.

Normalisation

SSADM uses full normalisation. This is done as an adjunct to and in confirmation of data modelling using graphical techniques. This is very laudable, and is no doubt well worth the effort when dealing with huge government projects such as the ones which insist on SSADM. That is what it was designed for. Normalisation, however, requires a great deal of effort to use effectively as a data analysis tool.

There is nothing to prevent a data analyst using full normalisation in this way — and the analyst of course must do so if the project sponsor insists on it. However, as has already been explained in the main text of this book, ER Modelling and a good understanding of the user's environment will always be sufficient to produce a working model which may then be enhanced and perfected with prototyping techniques. SSADM, unfortunately, is not designed for a primarily prototyping approach. Within the context of an SSADM project, then, normalisation may well be a necessary element.

Index

A

B

C

D

E